Cultural Science

Cultural Science

Applications of Artificial Social Intelligence

William Sims Bainbridge, PhD

BEP BUSINESS EXPERT PRESS

Cultural Science: Applications of Artificial Social Intelligence

Copyright © Business Expert Press, LLC, 2020.

Cover image licensed by Ingram Image, StockPhotoSecrets.com

Cover and interior design by Exeter Premedia Services Private Ltd., Chennai, India

First published in 2020 by
Business Expert Press, LLC
222 East 46th Street, New York, NY 10017
www.businessexpertpress.com

ISBN-13: 978-1-95152-758-7 (paperback)
ISBN-13: 978-1-95152-759-4 (e-book)

Business Expert Press Collaborative Intelligence Collection

Collection ISSN: 2691-1779 (print)
Collection ISSN: 2691-1795 (electronic)

First edition: 2020

10 9 8 7 6 5 4 3 2 1

Printed in the United States of America.

Abstract

During this time in history when the world is undergoing great and uncertain change, it is worth reconsidering the relationships connecting computer science, social science, and the humanities. One popular form of artificial social intelligence, namely recommender systems, can become a far more valuable tool for research on the arts, beginning with movies and computer games, then extending to all the other artforms. Survey research using questionnaires is well established, but social media offer great improvements in both methodology and application. It is time also for a revival of computer simulation as a tool for development of rigorous theories of social interaction, both abstractly and in human experience of virtual worlds. The study of literature is a major focus of education, yet it needs creative modernization, both to make use of computer collection and analysis of data, and to include the vast new online medium of millions of works of amateur fiction. Industry and an enthusiastic social movement have oversold pure artificial intelligence, as for example illustrated by AI's failure to understand poetry, and we must develop the best methods for human use of the new technology. Together, these developments offer opportunities and challenges for both industry and government policy. Unless artificial intelligence converges successfully with the social sciences and humanities, it will be justly accused of insincerity, exaggeration, extremely negative impacts, and subservience to the inhumane ambitions of technocrats and other societal elites.

Keywords

cultural science; artificial intelligence; human-computer interaction; converging technologies; recommender system; social media; games; literature

Contents

CHAPTER 1

Convergence of Humanities, Social Science, and Information Science

The world is undergoing a vast cultural transformation, involving globalization and communication via the World Wide Web, but also marked by the emergence of a vast number and diversity of online sub-cultures. The economic consequences are quite significant, not merely in the entertainment industries but in commerce more generally. In universities, the recent decline of enrollments in the humanities and the growth of enrollments in computer science suggest that tradi-tional definitions of academic fields may be obsolete, and innovation may revive the humanities by rendering them more computational. Since well over a century ago when Hollerith developed information technology to analyze the 1900 U.S. census, the social sciences have been relatively computational, but they also connect to the human-ities and thus can serve as agents of convergence.[1] Much public debate currently rages about possible unintended negative consequences of information technologies, such as artificial intelligence, and the efforts of computer science organizations and corporations to emphasize eth-ics would be greatly facilitated by partnership with the humanities and social sciences.

---

[1] Bainbridge, W.S. 2004. "Hollerith Card." In *Berkshire Encyclopedia of Human Computer Interaction*, ed. W.S. Bainbridge, 326–328. Great Barrington, Massachusetts: Berkshire Publishing Group.

The Convergence of Cultural Science

When *cognitive science* emerged some years ago, chiefly through convergence of artificial intelligence, cognitive psychology, and linguistics, two of the most cognitive sciences were not involved, sociology and political science, and the involvement of cultural anthropology was relatively minor. A logical explanation is that these fields involve social cognition, rather than the functioning of an individual mind, and they study real-world situations in which disagreement rather than consensus may reign. Of course, some forms of artificial intelligence are really social, notably multiagent systems, as are some related methodologies such as genetic algorithms. It is time for a new *cultural science* to develop, the younger sibling of cognitive science, through convergence of humanities, social sciences, and computer and information sciences. A key methodology to accomplish this will be *artificial social intelligence*.[2] When considering how to evaluate progress in artificial intelligence, Kenneth Forbus suggested, "the best approach is to evaluate AI systems by their ability to participate in our culture."[3] For this technology to strengthen rather than weaken human culture, the appropriate forms of convergence must be discovered.

Emerging out of the multidisciplinary National Nanotechnology Initiative, a series of conferences organized by the National Science Foundation explored in great depth "NBIC"—the convergence of Nanotechnology, Biotechnology, Information technology, and new technologies based on Cognitive science. A series of massive reports was published, starting in 2003 with *Converging Technologies for Improving Human Performance* and most recently in 2016 with *Handbook of Science and Technology Convergence*, chiefly edited by Bainbridge in collaboration

---

[2] Bainbridge, W.S., E.E. Brent, K. Carley, D.R. Heise, M.W. Macy, B. Markovsky, and J. Skvoretz. 1994. "Artificial Social Intelligence." *Annual Review of Sociology* 20, pp. 407–436.

[3] Forbus, K.D. 2016. "Software Social Organisms: Implications for Measuring AI Progress." *AI Magazine* 37, no. 1, pp. 85–90, p. 88.

with Mihail Roco, the leader of the National Nanotechnology Initiative.[4] A chapter introducing culture science proclaimed:

> Unification of the social sciences, and their greater integration into society, might be advanced significantly through the concept of *cultural science*. This is an emerging science of the shared concepts and practices of large social groups, based on convergence across sociology, political science, cultural anthropology, linguistics, and related fields. Cultural science takes its inspiration from cognitive science, but with the ambition to become a coequal partner in understanding and improving human behavior. As a metaphor, it considers any complex social system to be a "mind" or a "computer" that processes information and takes action, based on shared memory that is called *culture*. As a tool for achieving convergence of the social sciences, it is quite compatible with other unifying concepts, and only vigorous future research can determine its full potential.[5]

---

[4] Roco, M.C., and W.S. Bainbridge, eds. 2001. *Societal Implications of Nanoscience and Nanotechnology*. Dordrecht, Netherlands: Kluwer. Roco, M.C., and W.S. Bainbridge, eds. 2003. *Converging Technologies for Improving Human Performance*. Dordrecht, Netherlands: Kluwer; Roco, M.C., and Monemagno, C.D., eds. 2004. *The Coevolution of Human Potential and Converging Technologies*. New York, NY: New York Academy of Sciences. Roco, M.C., and W.S. Bainbridge, eds. 2006. *Nanotechnology: Societal Implications—Maximizing Benefit for Humanity*. Berlin: Springer; Bainbridge, W.S., and M.C. Roco, eds. 2006. *Progress in Convergence: Technologies for Human Wellbeing*. New York, NY: New York Academy of Sciences; Roco, M.C., W.S. Bainbridge, B. Tonn, and G. Whitesides, eds. 2016. *Convergence of Knowledge, Technology and Society*. Dordrecht, Netherlands: Springer; Bainbridge, W.S., and Roco, M.C., eds. 2016. *Handbook of Science and Technology Convergence*. Dordrecht, Netherlands: Springer.
[5] Bainbridge, W.S. 2016. "Cultural Science." In *Handbook of Science and Technology Convergence*, ed. W.S. Bainbridge and M.C. Roco, 767–779. Dordrecht, Netherlands: Springer.

In his contribution to the first NBIC conference in 2002, Jim Spohrer from IBM surveyed how many fields could advance in collaboration with each other, including this prediction concerning his own field:

> Information science advances will find many applications in the ongoing ebusiness transformation already underway, as well as pervasive communication and knowledge management tools to empower individuals. More importantly, information science will provide both the interlingua to knit the other technologies together and the raw computational power needed to store and manipulate mountains of new knowledge.[6]

He also saw key roles for social science:

> Social science advances (obtained from studies of real systems as well as simulations of complex adaptive systems composed of many interacting individuals) will provide fresh insights into the collective IQ of humans, as well as interspecies collective IQ and the spread of memes.

In the context of computer simulations of social behavior, the expression *collective IQ* is nearly equivalent to *artificial social intelligence*. His terms *interlingua* and *meme* both belong to cultural science.

Of course, Interlingua is a specific artificial language, which Wikipedia reports is actually used in some practical contexts as an auxiliary language and its "vocabulary, grammar and other characteristics are derived from natural languages, rather than being centrally planned."[7] Metaphorically, an *interlingua*, uncapitalized, is a set of concepts and terms drawn from two or more cultures or technical fields, adapted to some degree to serve as an effective tool for communicating convergently. An example of

---

[6] Spohrer, J. 2003. "Opportunities and Challenges." In *Converging Technologies for Improving Human Performance*, eds. M.C. Roco and W.S. Bainbridge, 101–117. Dordrecht, Netherlands: Kluwer. www.wtec.org/ConvergingTechnologies/Report/NBIC_report.pdf

[7] en.wikipedia.org/wiki/Interlingua

an interlingua term is indeed *meme*, which Wikipedia defines as "a unit for carrying cultural ideas, symbols, or practices, that can be transmitted from one mind to another through writing, speech, gestures, rituals, or other imitable phenomena with a mimicked theme."[8] The word *meme* is itself a convergence of biological and cultural terminology, based on biological *gene* and social *imitation*.[9]

I had long been interested in the parallels and differences between genetic and cultural evolution, and at a 1982 conference I gave a paper that noted the limitations as well as the advantages of the memetic approach:

> In order for a cultural genetics to be possible, three things are necessary: First, there must be some process of reproduction and inheritance, in which cultural structures and elements are transmitted from one "generation" to the next. Second, there must be a significant measure of stability in the transmission process, in which the replicators show sufficient copying-fidelity to transmit recognizable patterns. Third, there must be some process such as sexuality or mutation which introduces change and variety into the process of inheritance yet is sufficiently coherent itself to permit scientific analysis. In fact these conditions are met by religious cults and by at least some other phenomena such as stylistic schools in the various arts. If other parts of the wider culture fail to exhibit these features, still there will be an "inorganic chemistry" of culture if not the full richness of an organic genetics, and the rules of one can illuminate the rules of the other.[10]

Cults were a good example, because there is an extensive historical and ethnographic record of thousands of them, so they can serve as the cultural equivalent of the bacteria on which geneticists invested much early research effort, prior to the development of gene sequencing technologies.

---

8 en.wikipedia.org/wiki/Meme
9 Dawkins, R. 1976. *The Selfish Gene*. New York, NY: Oxford University Press.
10 Bainbridge, W.S. 1985. "Cultural Genetics." In *Religious Movements*, ed. Rodney Stark, 157–198. New York, NY: Paragon.

Now Internet gives us research access to vast numbers and diversities of much larger cultures.

At the first NBIC conference, Gary Strong and I explored the possible development of what we then called "Memetics: A Potential New Science," with this preface:

> In the "information society" of the 21st century, the most valuable resource will not be iron or oil but culture. However, the sciences of human culture have lacked a formal paradigm and a rigorous methodology. A fresh approach to culture, based on biological metaphors and information science methodologies, could vastly enhance the human and economic value of our cultural heritage and provide cognitive science with a host of new research tools.[11]

As this book will amply illustrate, biology is not the only source of concepts for cultural science, and naturally many branches of the social sciences will contribute as well. In my own work, social networks have been especially significant, and the concluding chapter of my new book *The Social Structure of Online Communities* begins:

> The emergence of online communities provides a platform where a new multidisciplinary field of science can be assembled from portions of many existing disciplines: cultural science. The analogy is with cognitive science, that emerged over recent decades, and it contains several rather accurate metaphors. If cognitive science concerns how the individual mind works, on the basis of the structure and dynamics of the brain, then cultural science will concern how social structures create and sustain shared concepts, genres of art or literature, and technologies. If neural networks are the primary mechanism by which the individual mind works, then social networks serve the same role for culture, and sociomet-

---

[11] Strong, G., and W.S. Bainbridge. 2003. "Memetics: A Potential New Science." In *Converging Technologies for Improving Human Performance*, edited by M.C. Roco and W.S. Bainbridge, 318–325. Dordrecht, Netherlands: Kluwer, www. wtec.org/ConvergingTechnologies/Report/NBIC_report.pdf

ric methods are fundamental for cultural science. At the current moment in history, many of the essential components of cultural science already exist, but often separated from each other in different college departments, or in various computer-related industries or informal online communities.[12]

My partner in the many convergence conferences and publications, Mihail Roco of the Engineering Directorate of the National Science Foundation, has very clearly explained that convergence is not the only process that will drive future progress, because *divergence* is also important. To return to the biological example, evolution is not merely graduate improvement of the adaptation of a particular species, but also speciation, a split of a gene pool into two or more new species that become independent of each other. In our 2016 *Handbook of Science and Technology Convergence*, he wrote:

> The convergence-divergence cycle is a typical process in science and technology (S&T) development. It consists of four phases: (A) creative assembling of contributions from multiple fields leading to new concepts or ideas, (B) system integration leading to a new assembly or invention for known uses, (C) technological innovation outputs leading to new products and applications, and (D) spin-off outcomes that lead to solutions not possible before and that produce new competencies, tools, and applications. Each cycle and each phase generally follow each other in a quasi-exponential growth pattern.[13]

Cultural science must comprehend the convergence–divergence dynamic, must not assert one single framework for thought and judgment, and

---

[12] Bainbridge, W.S. *The Social Structure of Online Communities*. Cambridge, England: Cambridge University Press, 2020.

[13] Roco, M.C. 2016. "Convergence-Divergence Process." In *Handbook of Science and Technology Convergence*, ed. W.S. Bainbridge and M.C. Roco, 79–94. Dordrecht, Netherlands: Springer.

thus must draw deeply from the humanities, which are often intelligent but relatively incoherent.

Humanistic Scholarship

In the context of the convergence–divergence dynamic, cultural science faces two distinctive challenges. The first is the principle emphasized by cultural anthropologists over the past century: *cultural relativism*.[14] This term has several possible meanings or degrees of emphasis, but a central idea is that no one culture is superior to all the others, each perhaps being an equally valid adaptation to the natural and historical conditions under which it arose. That raises the issue of moral relativity, and today many anthropologists seek to distance their discipline from it.[15] Does each system of morality apply only to members of the society that preaches it? In sociology, a distinction was made between *particularism*, which respects the right of each culture to favor its own members and establish rules that function to their advantage, versus *universalism* that applies the same abstract moral code to all human beings.[16] The hope of the New World Order that followed the end of the Soviet Union was that universalism would reign supreme, but today within nations as well as around the globe we see revival of particularism.

Among philosophers, politicians, and the general public, there have been endless debates about where we must seek our moral principles. A traditional answer was from religion, but in ancient days when large pantheons of gods represented competing natural principles and tribes, a stable basis for judgment other than particularism was lacking. When Moses ascended Mount Sinai and returned with a clear set of commandments, the ethical advantage of monotheism became obvious. But for centuries western societies have sought a secular basis for morality. Thomas Hobbes

---

[14] Herskovits, M.J. 1958. "Some Further Comments on Cultural Relativism." *American Anthropologist* 60, no. 2, pp. 266–273.

[15] Perusek, D. 2007. "Grounding Cultural Relativism." *Anthropological Quarterly* 80, no. 3, pp. 821–836; Brown, M.F. 2008. "Cultural Relativism 2.0." *Current Anthropology* 49, no. 3, pp. 363–383.

[16] Parsons, T., and Shils, E.A. eds. 1951. *Toward a General Theory of Action.* Cambridge, Massachusetts: Harvard University Press.

(1588–1679) and Jean-Jacques Rousseau (1712–1778) offered different versions of *social contract* theory, arguing that morality was necessary for human welfare, and thus required the members of a society to come to some agreement about what the rules should be.[17] This abandoned any transcendental conception of ethics, and supported the development of democratic institutions through which a consensus could be achieved. However, any particular rule may benefit some people at a cost to other people, and our current world seems to be falling away from agreement toward conflicts along many fracture lines.[18]

The second distinctive challenge for cultural science is the difficulty in achieving consensus on its own concepts, research methods, and empirical findings. This problem may be more than merely the application of cultural relativism to cultural science itself, although that is certainly a factor. In this book we shall encounter many schools of thought that were influential within one or another social science during the 20th century, but only a subset is popular today. Those that faded in importance were not really disproven, but seemed increasingly less rewarding to academics or entrepreneurs under changing conditions of technology, economy, and their student or consumer clientele. We may hope that a new surge of research innovation will finally find the ultimate truths about human life and society, and modest efforts like writing or reading this book may help achieve that lofty goal, but it may not be possible soon if ever.

This book will illustrate the value of a variety of quantitative methods largely drawn from statistical social science. Both *value* and *variety* are important qualifications. Yes, the failure of the humanities to use mathematics extensively has limited their value and relevance to the modern, computerized world. But the great variety of existing statistical methods will only increase as we apply them to more and more genres in the arts and literature, thus giving researchers a good deal of freedom to decide which method to use for what purpose in each context. Here we shall

---

[17] Hobbes, T. 1651. *Leviathan, or, The Matter, Forme, and Power of a Commonwealth Ecclesiasticall and Civil.* London: Crooke; R. Jean-Jacques. 1893 [1762]. *The Social Contract: or, Principles of Political Law.* New York, NY: Eckler.

[18] Fischer, C.S., and G. Mattson. 2009. "Is America Fragmenting?" *Annual Review of Sociology* 35, pp. 435–455.

often suggest formal hypotheses about the structure and dynamics of culture, but we are relatively seldom testing hypotheses. Rather, we are engaged in exploration, using statistics as the coordinates with which to draw maps of culture. However, even though latitude and longitude are well defined, the variables drawn on a map may vary greatly, and one may emphasize mountains while another emphasizes the roads that go around them. One way to consider this is that in cultural science the *unit of analysis* depends upon the available information and the goal of the researcher. Consider this sentence:

> Tyrion Lannister knew the maps as well as anyone, but a fortnight on the wild track that passed for the kingsroad up here had brought home the lesson that the map was one thing and the land quite another.

At this point the unit of analysis is the sentence. But this is the second sentence of a book chapter, and phrases like "chapter and verse" remind us that literature arranges words in complex structures, and each level of the structure can be the unit of analysis. Sometimes the words will be the units of interest, such as the use of the archaic or anglophile mathematical measure *fortnight*. In this case the book is part of a series, so the series could be the unit of analysis, or indeed the author could be. Given their form and position in the sentence, the words *Tyrion Lannister* seem to name a person, and we may wonder who he or she might be. Today it is easy to find out, because Tyrion Lannister has his own Wikipedia page, which says:

> Tyrion is a dwarf and member of House Lannister of Casterly Rock, one of the wealthiest and most powerful families in the fictional continent of Westeros. In the story, Tyrion uses his status as a Lannister to mitigate the prejudice he has received all of his life, even from his family. Knowing that no one will ever take him seriously, he soothes his inadequacies with wine, wit and self-indulgence. As the peaceful rule of King Robert Baratheon begins to decay, Tyrion sees how ill-equipped his family are to hold everything together. He first saves his own neck from the

vengeful Catelyn Stark and her sister Lysa Arryn, then is sent by his father Tywin to impose order on the capital of King's Landing, as well as his nephew Joffrey, the new king, as civil war begins.[19]

So, Tyrion's map concerns a *fictional continent*, and he must be a character in literature. This does not mean he is insignificant, because in its associated history page Wikipedia reports that Tyrion's page received 200,084 views in the period from April 21 through May 11, 2019, and fully 3,016,112 pageviews since the counting began on July 1, 2015. The paragraph above refers to social units of analysis bigger than the individual, notably the general term *family* and the more specific feudal phrase *House Lannister*. As it happens, the title of the chapter in which the quoted sentence appears is "Tyrion" and the edition of that book I have includes an extensive appendix describing the main houses of Westeros, each of which has a motto that expresses the core concept of its family culture: (1) Lannister: "Hear Me Roar," (2) Baratheon: "Ours Is the Fury," (3) Arryn: "As High as Honor," (4) Stark: "Winter Is Coming." I placed House Stark last in this list because of its close connection to political reality. Of course everybody knows that I co-authored three books with a real-life member of House Stark, namely sociologist of religion Rodney Stark, their cultural character illustrated by the fact that one was translated into Polish and another into Chinese.[20] But an even more powerful connection to reality is the fact that Donald Trump, president of the United States, explicitly mimicked "Winter is Coming," using the phrase "Sanctions Are Coming" in a tweet and poster of himself "to announce that his administration would be reimposing economic sanctions on Iran."[21] I will leave

---

[19] en.wikipedia.org/wiki/Tyrion_Lannister

[20] Stark, R., and W.S. Bainbridge. 1985. *The Future of Religion*. Berkeley: University of California Press. [translated into Chinese, 2006, China Renmin University Press], Stark, R., and W.S. Bainbridge. 1987. *A Theory of Religion*. New York, NY: Toronto/Lang. [translated into Polish, 2000, Krakow: Nomos], *Religion, Deviance and Social Control* (New York: Routledge, 1996).

[21] Brewer, L. 2019. "Trump's 'Game of Thrones'-Style Poster Makes Cryptic Cameo at Cabinet Meeting." *Washington Post*, January 2, 2019, www.washingtonpost.com/politics/2019/01/02/trumps-game-thrones-style-poster-makes-cryptic-cameo-cabinet-meeting/

to partisans and political scientists to report what motto describes the cultural values of House Trump.

The Wikipedia page for Tyrion Lannister naturally links to the page for George R.R. Martin, the author who invented him, which earned 672,453 pageviews since April 21, 2019, and 8,923,474 since July 1, 2015.[22] The sentence came from Martin's novel *A Game of Thrones*, and the recent interest in him and Tyrion was generated by the fact that the HBO television series based on the series titled *Game of Thrones* was nearing its conclusion. As I write this in the afternoon of May 12, 2019, we do not yet know if Tyrion Lannister will survive the battle that is predicted to begin on the world's television sets this evening, but we can report that the Wikipedia page for the TV series had earned 3,451,842 pageviews since April 21, 2019, and 53,855,873 since July 1, 2015.[23] However, the mere popularity of this component of modern world culture is not the reason I quoted the particular sentence that expressed the thoughts of a nonexistent person. I happened to be familiar with the lineage of its main idea. Tyrion Lannister got it from George R.R. Martin, and probably Martin got it from A.E. van Vogt who definitely got it from Alfred Korzybski.

Like Martin early in his career, A.E. van Vogt (1912–2000) was a science fiction writer, and later we shall glimpse how he fit into the science-fiction literary subculture from which Martin emigrated into the more profitable and perhaps creative pseudo-historical fantasy genre represented by J.R.R. Tolkien. But googling "Tyrion Lannister Korzybski" turned up a few examples of accurate links. A post on TVTropes, "the all devouring pop-culture wiki," offered this interpretation:

> At the beginning of Tyrion's second chapter, he makes reference to Alfred Korzybski's famous postmodern axiom, "The map is not the territory." In a nutshell, it warns people against confusing their idealistic idea of how reality works—for instance, believing that

---

[22] en.wikipedia.org/wiki/George_R._R._Martin
[23] en.wikipedia.org/wiki/Game_of_Thrones

acting honorably will always get you rewarded—with the nihilistic moral void of real life.[24]

The phrase "nihilistic moral void" seems an accurate description of Westeros, and we may worry that it also applies to our real world, at a time in history when optimism is in retreat. A post on A Forum of Ice and Fire gave a different example from Martin's books: "'The map is not the land, my father often said.' (A Dance with Dragons—Jon IV) 'The map is not the territory'—Alfred Korzybski."[25] The reference the erudite poster put in parentheses tells us that the quotation came from the fourth chapter named "Jon" after its main character, Jon Snow, in the fifth novel of the series *A Dance with Dragons*.[26]

Wikipedia explains:

> The map-territory relation describes the relationship between an object and a representation of that object, as in the relation between a geographical territory and a map of it. Polish-American scientist and philosopher Alfred Korzybski remarked that "the map is not the territory" and that "the word is not the thing", encapsulating his view that an abstraction derived from something, or a reaction to it, is not the thing itself. Korzybski held that many people do confuse maps with territories, that is, confuse models of reality with reality itself.[27]

Korzybski believed that awareness of this truth would liberate people, probably to become more rather than less moral, and in the science fiction context it suggested that intentionally reorganizing our minds could render us super-human. We shall not adopt that theory here, but it illustrates how literature and philosophy can seek transcendence from limitations of ordinary life, and we can seek connections between literature and philosophy by means of online search engines.

---

[24] tvtropes.org/pmwiki/pmwiki.php/YMMV/AGameOfThrones

[25] asoiaf.westeros.org/index.php?/profile/58452-shadowcat-rivers/conten

[26] Martin, G.R.R. 2011. *A Dance with Dragons*, 251. New York: Bantam.

[27] en.wikipedia.org/wiki/Map%E2%80%93territory_relation

Conclusion

In several senses, cultural science is not new. A group of scholars chiefly located in Australia established a journal with that title to serve as

> the home of a community of scholars drawn from natural and social sciences, as well as the humanities. We want to understand how cultural systems function, how culture creates the groups that create knowledge, and how that operates at global scale.[28]

In his 1998 book, *The Freudian Calling*, Louis Rose argued strenuously that psychoanalytic interpretations of society should be specifically categorized as a particular school of thought within cultural science.[29] In his contribution "Software Cultures," to the 2004 encyclopedia I edited, *Human-Computer Interaction*, Václav Rajlich explained:

> Communities of programmers develop and maintain software artifacts. Like other human communities, they develop distinct cultures. During the history of software technology, there have been many different, identifiable software cultures, each of which has had a distinct set of characteristics.[30]

Thus, there will be many subdisciplines and schools of thought within the cultural science of the future, including *cultural computer science.*

---

[28] culturalscience.org/about

[29] Rose, L. 1998. *The Freudian Calling*, 19. Detroit: Wayne State University Press.

[30] Rajlich, V. 2004. "Software Cultures." In *Encyclopedia of Human-Computer Interaction*, ed. W.S. Bainbridge, 659–663. Great Barrington, Massachusetts: Berkshire.

CHAPTER 2

Recommender Systems as a Collaborative Form of ASI

Artificial social intelligence is much broader than mere multiagent systems, whether the agents are represented by neural nets or rule-based systems, involving many kinds of partnership between humans and machines. A powerful and well-established example is recommender systems, which are not popularly called AI yet typically involve machine learning of some form, analyzing preferences or behaviors of people in order, commonly, to advise them what movie or other cultural product they might want to experience next.[1] A good example is the classic 2006 Netflix dataset of ratings of 17,770 movies by hundreds of thousands of its customers. When computer scientists work on recommender systems, they tend to seek to improve the predictive power of the algorithms, which serves the financial interests of the vendor company that acquired the data and offers good advice to the customers. However, it is relatively rare for such data to be used in the humanities to map the current structure and historical dynamics of cinema cultures or other subcultures interested in particular

---

[1] Goldberg, D., D. Nichols, B.M. Oki, and D. Terry. 1992. "Using Collaborative Filtering to Weave an Information Tapestry." *Communications of the ACM* 35, no. 12, pp. 61–70; Resnick, P., and H.R. Varian. 1997. "Recommender Systems." *Communications of the ACM* 40, no. 3, pp. 56–58; Basu, C., H. Hirsh, and W. Cohen. 1998. "Recommendation as Classification: Using Social and Content-Based Information in Recommendation." In *Proceedings of the Fifteenth National Conference on Artificial Intelligence.* Madison, Wisconsin; Canny, C. 2002. "Collaborative Filtering with Privacy via Factor Analysis." In *Proceedings of the 25th Annual International ACM SIGIR Conference on Research and Development in Information Retrieval,* 238–245. New York, NY: ACM; Herlocker, J.L., J.A. Konstan, L.G. Terveen, and J.T. Riedl. 2004. "Evaluating Collaborative Filtering Recommender Systems." *ACM Transactions on Information Systems* 22, pp. 5–53.

artistic genres. This topic is good for the second chapter of this book for three reasons: (1) it offers clear examples of principles that will feature in later chapters, (2) the field of research is well but unevenly developed, such that research priorities can be proposed with some confidence, and (3) it has obvious relevance in both economic profits for the media companies and educational benefits for a range of college and precollege academic subjects.

Systems for Recommending Movies

Since the very beginning of the 20th century, motion pictures have been a major segment of popular culture and an economically significant industry. Arguably, the technology became technically mature by the year 1939, with the release of high-quality sound and color films, notably *The Wizard of Oz* and *Gone with the Wind*. Computer-generated graphics have facilitated some improvement in special effects, especially for fantasy and science-fiction films, but occasional technological fads like 3D have not led to radical reformulation of the medium over the past eight decades. However, Internet and cable streaming services have liberated audiences from theaters and allowed them to view what they wanted when they wanted. For example, anyone can invest the 12 minutes required to view the 1903 classic short *The Great Train Robbery* in any of several copies freely available on YouTube. To get a sense of its historical context, one may search the old newspapers at the Chronicling America online digital library of the U.S. Library of Congress, for example, finding this notice on the May 26, 1904 front page of *The Morning Appeal* newspaper in Carson City, Nevada: "The great train robbery, the finest film yet shown at the Vitagraph will be shown for the last time this evening."[2] A much more recent evaluation of this pioneering work of action-oriented art can be found on its Wikipedia page, which had been viewed 384,761 times in the period July 1, 2015, through March 12, 2019.[3]

Before we consider how today's revolutionary communication media are either fragmenting or unifying popular culture, we need both an

---

[2] chroniclingamerica.loc.gov
[3] en.wikipedia.org/wiki/The_Great_Train_Robbery_(1903_film)

historical perspective and a sense of the technical features of well-established methods for mapping a cultural genre. The Internet Movie Database (IMDb) classifies *The Great Train Robbery* as "short, action, crime" or "short, western," depending upon which of two editions one checks.[4] IMDb links to two sources of judgment: published reviews by professional movie critics and ratings plus descriptions from ordinary users of the Metacritic online information service. Those are really the traditional sources that audiences relied upon to decide whether to see a film: (1) professional critics who published in the local newspaper or elsewhere and (2) neighbors who had seen the film and commented privately about it. While there are various methods to draw insights from traditional sources, modern recommender systems often gather their own information in a manner similar to social-science questionnaire survey research. A total of 15,258 IMDb users rated *The Great Train Robbery* on a scale from 1 to 10, the modal response being 7, which 31.6 percent of them selected. If we had data on how the same users rated many other films, we could use statistical methods to identify clusters of films having similar characteristics, such as westerns. To illustrate this approach, we need a different database.

In August 1978, I took a carload of paper questionnaires of two types to the 36th annual World Science Fiction Convention in Phoenix, Arizona. The main part of this research project sought to map the cultural structure of science fiction literature, and its questionnaire asked respondents to rate 140 authors and many types of literature described in standard terms used by critics who published in the popular science fiction magazines. There were five versions of this questionnaire, listing the authors in different random orders to avoid correlations simply because of the placement of the names, and two of the authors were fake names to catch frivolous responders. The data were manually entered into Hollerith style computer cards, and I wrote programs to rearrange the data about authors in the same order. Factor analysis of the data did an excellent job in identifying four main subcultures of science fiction literature: (1) hard-science SF that was logical and based on the physical sciences,

---

4 www.imdb.com/title/tt0000439; www.imdb.com/title/tt0000487

(2) new-wave SF that was more poetic and connected to social science, (3) a cluster of types of SF-related fantasy including horror and "sword-and-sorcery," and (4) classic SF of its early days headed by the works of Jules Verne and H.G. Wells. The results were published as a book from Harvard University Press.[5]

The second questionnaire was more problematic, focusing on 67 movies the attendees at the convention were likely to have seen, asking them to rate each on a 7-point scale from 0 (do not like) to 6 (like very much). For the analysis reported here, I focused on the 200 respondents who had rated at least 45 of the 67 movies, and a general issue for cultural survey research is the degree of familiarity the respondents have with the topic. Again, one of the main methodologies was factor analysis. Wikipedia correctly describes this approach and connects it to modern artificial intelligence:

> Factor analysis is a statistical method used to describe variability among observed, correlated variables in terms of a potentially lower number of unobserved variables called factors ... Factor analysis aims to find independent latent variables. It is a theory used in machine learning and related to data mining.[6]

But it is not a new method, and was largely developed by Charles Spearman (1863–1945) nearly a century ago.[7]

The most central connection of factor analysis to modern machine learning is that it is an iterative process, many stages of which can be either automated or decided by the human user. In my analysis of the 1978 movie data, I instructed the computer to rotate the factors, which meant that it automatically went through a series of iterations to improve the clarity of the analysis. I had the option of telling it how many factors to seek, or to follow the statistical criterion of all factors with eigenvalues greater than 1. In much more recent online research, I administered Lewis

[5]   Bainbridge, W.S. 1986. *Dimensions of Science Fiction*. Cambridge: Harvard University Press.

[6]   en.wikipedia.org/wiki/Factor_analysis

[7]   en.wikipedia.org/wiki/Charles_Spearman

Goldberg's set of 100 questionnaire items measuring the so-called Big Five personality dimensions to 3,267 respondents, vastly more than such studies usually have, and thus potentially strengthening the reliability of the statistics.[8] I ran two different factor analyses. In a *confirmatory analysis*, I told the statistical analysis software to do a common kind of principal component analysis with rotation, calling for five factors, and pretty exactly I got the Big Five. Then I compared an *exploratory analysis*, with everything the same, but asking for as many factors that had eigenvalues greater than 1. That produced fully 15 factors.[9] Even though the 100 questionnaire items had been designed to measure exactly five dimensions, the human responses had a more complex structure. A system that automatically experimented with a range of criteria, from rotation to varying eigenvalues to selection of subsets of items for further analysis, would clearly identify factor analysis as a form of machine learning.

Other options illustrated with the 1978 movie data are focusing on a subset of more knowledgeable respondents and on films that have characteristics in common. Table 2.1 reports results of an analysis of the 36 best-known movies, 17 of which clustered well into 3 factors. The most popular film for the 1978 respondents was *Star Wars* (1977), seen by all the respondents and rated an average of 5.45 on the 0 to 6 scale, but it did not fall into any particular factor. While the movies are more than four decades old, they are relevant today, as demonstrated by the large numbers of times people have viewed their Wikipedia articles, data covering the period from July 1, 2015, through March 12, 2019. Notably, the 1939 classic *The Wizard of Oz* attracted fully 6,192,237 recent *pageviews*.

Factor analysis takes a correlation matrix as its input, and the output includes new scores for the items, called *loadings*, that are rather like

---

[8]   Goldberg, L.R. 1993. "The Structure of Phenotypic Personality Traits." *American Psychologist* 48, pp. 26–34, Goldberg, L.R. 1999. "A Broad-Bandwidth, Public Domain, Personality Inventory Measuring the Lower-Level Facets of Several Five-Factor Models." In *Personality Psychology in Europe*, eds. I. Mervielde, I. Deary, F. De Fruyt, and F. Ostendorf, Vol 7, 7–28. Tilburg University Press, Tilburg, Netherlands.

[9]   Bainbridge, W.S. 2012. "Whole-Personality Emulation." *International Journal of Machine Consciousness* 4, no. 1, pp. 159–175, Bainbridge, W.S. 2014. *Personality Capture and Emulation*, 58–62. London: Springer.

Table 2.1 Factor analysis of old but popular movies

	Year	Mean Score	Percent Rated	Factor 1 Loading	Factor 2 Loading	Factor 3 Loading	2015–2019 Wikipedia Pageviews
			1978 SF Convention Questionnaire Data				
Factor 1							
Logan's Run	1976	3.31	96.5%	0.67	–0.04	–0.05	1,539,820
Soylent Green	1973	3.50	93.0%	0.61	0.12	0.04	2,798,725
The Andromeda Strain	1971	4.59	98.0%	0.59	–0.02	0.07	460,597
The Omega Man	1971	3.31	91.5%	0.58	–0.10	–0.05	769,621
Westworld	1973	3.89	95.5%	0.57	0.11	0.03	1,437,308
Fantastic Voyage	1966	4.00	98.0%	0.52	–0.14	0.12	509,048
The Land That Time Forgot	1974	2.49	88.5%	0.50	0.16	0.05	245,642
Factor 2							
Psycho	1960	4.18	88.0%	–0.11	0.68	–0.02	5,320,274
The Bride of Frankenstein	1935	3.42	87.5%	–0.06	0.65	0.29	922,810
Rosemary's Baby	1968	2.62	88.0%	0.02	0.59	0.12	2,769,900
The Fly	1958	2.76	90.5%	0.15	0.59	0.16	480,875
King Kong	1933	4.56	98.0%	0.01	0.54	0.33	1,537,859
Invasion of the Body Snatchers	1956	4.19	88.0%	0.12	0.51	0.16	842,633
Factor 3:							
20,000 Leagues Under the Sea	1954	4.16	97.0%	0.10	0.14	0.68	825,987
Forbidden Planet	1956	5.09	99.0%	0.00	0.08	0.60	1,036,063
The Wizard of Oz	1939	4.47	99.0%	–0.18	0.30	0.54	6,192,237
The Day the Earth Stood Still	1951	5.25	97.5%	0.11	0.07	0.52	1,118,914

correlations between the item and each of the latent factors. Table 2.1 uses a somewhat arbitrary criterion, including only films that loaded at least 0.50 on one of the factors. In most cases, a film has one big loading, and the other two are statistically indistinguishable from 0, reflecting a very successful factor analysis. The interesting exceptions are *The Bride of Frankenstein* (loaded 0.65 on factor 2 and 0.29 on factor 3), *King Kong*

(0.54 on factor 2 and 0.33 on factor 3), and *The Wizard of Oz* (0.30 on factor 2 and 0.54 on factor 3). A film that did not meet the 0.50 criterion for inclusion, *The Creature from the Black Lagoon*, loaded 0.20, 0.47, and 0.39. While in applications like the Big Five personality dimensions, in which items that load on multiple factors were excluded from the design of the instrument, when we study natural cultures we need to realize that a table like Table 2.1 is mapping films into a multidimensional conceptual space, rather than clustering the films, strictly speaking.

In the questionnaire rating science fiction authors, it worked very well to employ an extension of the factor analysis method, generating factor scores that could then be correlated with the respondent's ratings of the main terms used by critics to describe different subgenres or aspects of science fiction literature. This resulted in very solid descriptions of the meanings of all four main factors. That approach did not work as well for the movies, perhaps because the questionnaire was not based on very clear categorization schemes developed by knowledgeable film critics, and the subculture of science fiction fans was primarily oriented toward the literature. Indeed, cultures vary in terms of how solidly based they are upon clear ontologies.

How can we describe each of the three movie factors? From the dates, factor 1 clusters films that were very recent in 1978 when the questionnaire was administered, and their mean release date was 1972. The other two factors are older, with mean dates of 1952 and 1950. It is noteworthy that very high majorities of the respondents had seen each of the films, but that testifies to their relevance for the science fiction subculture, and today movies of all vintages are far more accessible to the general public than they were four decades ago. The third factor stands out in terms of their ratings, having an average of 4.7 on the 0 to 6 scale, while the other two factors were essentially tied at 3.6.

Having seen all the films in the table, I was aware that the factor 1 films were not merely similar in vintage but also in theme, each exploring an imagined, exotic environment. The right-hand column of the table suggests how anyone could learn their topics and other features, because all have their own article on Wikipedia, nine of them having been viewed over a million times in the period reported in their Wikipedia pageviews statistic. Here is how Wikipedia describes the factor 1 films:

Logan's Run "depicts a utopian future society on the surface, revealed as a dystopia where the population and the consumption of resources are maintained in equilibrium by killing everyone who reaches the age of thirty."[10]

Soylent Green "combines both police procedural and science fiction genres; the investigation into the murder of a wealthy businessman and a dystopian future of dying oceans and year-round humidity due to the greenhouse effect, resulting in suffering from pollution, poverty, overpopulation, euthanasia and depleted resources."[11]

The Andromeda Strain is a "science fiction thriller film" about "a team of scientists who investigate a deadly organism of extraterrestrial origin" "near the small rural town of Piedmont, New Mexico, almost all of the town's inhabitants die quickly."[12]

The Omega Man is about "a survivor of a global pandemic" who "spends his days patrolling the now-desolate Los Angeles, hunting and killing members of 'the Family', a cult of plague victims who were turned into nocturnal albino mutants."[13]

Westworld explores "a high-tech, highly realistic adult amusement park ... The resort's three 'worlds' are populated with lifelike androids that are practically indistinguishable from human beings, each programmed in character for their assigned historical environment."[14]

Fantastic Voyage follows "a submarine crew who are shrunk to microscopic size and venture into the body of an injured scientist to repair damage to his brain."[15]

The Land That Time Forgot explores "an uncharted sub-continent called Caprona, a fantastical land of lush vegetation where dinosaurs still roam, co-existing with primitive man."[16]

[10]   en.wikipedia.org/wiki/Logan%27s_Run_(film)

[11]   en.wikipedia.org/wiki/Soylent_Green

[12]   en.wikipedia.org/wiki/The_Andromeda_Strain_(film)

[13]   en.wikipedia.org/wiki/The_Omega_Man

[14]   en.wikipedia.org/wiki/Westworld_(film)

[15]   en.wikipedia.org/wiki/Fantastic_Voyage

[16]   en.wikipedia.org/wiki/The_Land_That_Time_Forgot_(1975_film)

Clearly, these themes harmonize with standard science fiction literature, but in fact there are also direct connections, *Fantastic Voyage* with
a novel by Isaac Asimov, *The Land That Time Forgot* with one by Edgar
Rice Burroughs, and *Logan's Run* with a novel written collaboratively by
William F. Nolan and George Clayton Johnson. *The Omega Man* was
based on the 1954 novel *I Am Legend* by Richard Matheson, about which
Wikipedia correctly reports:

> It was influential in the development of the zombie-vampire genre
> and in popularizing the concept of a worldwide apocalypse due
> to disease. The novel was a success and was adapted into the films
> *The Last Man on Earth* (1964), *The Omega Man* (1971), and *I
> Am Legend* (2007). It was also an inspiration behind *Night of the
> Living Dead* (1968).[17]

Not only was *Soylent Green* based on the 1966 novel *Make Room! Make
Room!* by Harry Harrison, but it was like a sequel to *The Omega Man*,
starring the same actor, Charlton Heston, and having one of the same
producers, Walter Seltzer. Novelist Michael Crichton wrote the stories
for both *Westworld* and *The Andromeda Strain*. Clearly, the films in factor
1 represent a subculture of science fiction literature that converged with
the movies.

While not defined as a recommender system, Wikipedia can easily
serve as an advisor about which movie one might next want to see. For
example, *Logan's Run*, *Soylent Green*, and *Omega Man* are included in
its list of *dystopian films*, so that seeing one could encourage viewing the
other two or indeed becoming a fan of the entire genre.[18] Many other
current online information sources about the film industry are relevant
to recommender systems, notably the IMDb that links to reviews by professional critics and reports ratings by users.[19] The IMDb page for *Logan's
Run* headlines a brief synopsis: "An idyllic science fiction future has one

---

[17] en.wikipedia.org/wiki/I_Am_Legend_(novel)

[18] en.wikipedia.org/wiki/Category:Dystopian_films

[19] www.metacritic.com/

major drawback: life must end at the age of thirty."[20] The average meta-score is rather low, just 53 on a scale of 1 to 100, but IMDb highlighted four reviews linked via Metacritic that had much higher scores:[21]

> Variety (metascore = 90): "*Logan's Run* is a rewarding futuristic film that appeals both as spectacular-looking escapist adventure as well as intelligent drama."

> Chicago Sun-Times, Roger Ebert (metascore = 75): "*Logan's Run* is a vast, silly extravaganza that delivers a certain amount of fun, once it stops taking itself seriously."

> The New York Times, Vincent Canby (metascore = 70): "*Logan's Run* is less interested in logic than in gadgets and spectacle, but these are sometimes jazzily effective and even poetic. Had more attention been paid to the screenplay, the movie might have been a stunner."

> IGN (metascore = 70): "Taken for what it is, *Logan's Run* delivers a fun ride and a glimpse at another era, even if it's probably not the time frame the producers had in mind."

The phrase "escapist adventure as well as intelligent drama" illustrates a challenge that in some form may be faced by cultural science in all areas: Which cultural features are relevant to a particular analysis, serving its goals rather than distracting from them? We have not emphasized that 5 of the 17 movies were filmed in black and white, rather than color. All of the factor 1 films could be described as *escapist*, because they venture far away from ordinary life. Yet one of the proverbs of SF fandom is: "Science fiction is escape ... into reality." By this the fans mean that popular culture ignores key truths about the nature of humans and the universe they inhabit. The term *intelligent* may refer to the asking of questions as much as answering. This returns us to the key theme of *cultural relativism*:

---

[20]   www.imdb.com/title/tt0074812
[21]   www.imdb.com/title/tt0074812/criticreviews

The criteria used to map the structure of a culture are themselves cultural products, so very different analyses may be equally valid.

Table 2.2 summarizes the IMDb and Metacritic information about the three factors of films rated by the 1978 science fiction convention, chiefly based on new data but including a few of the original movie reviews. The Metacritic scores are on a 1 to 100 scale, while the IMDb user scores are on a 1 to 10 scale. Interestingly, IMDb reports the gender of most user reviewers. In the case of *Logan's Run*, of 46,894 raters, 33,178 self-identified as male and 4,252 as female. Thus, only 11.4 percent of the 37,430 who reported their gender were female. The highest percent female, 26.7, is for *The Wizard of Oz* in which a heroine explores a fantasy world, and the second-highest, 22.2 percent, is for *Rosemary's Baby*. We may weigh the balance between two hypotheses: (1) users of IMDb who report their gender are predominantly male and (2) female users of IMDb are less interested in science fiction than are male users.

Table 2.2 Data about three sci-fi factors at the Internet movie database

	Metacritic Score (1–100)	User Score (1–10)	Users Who Rated It	Percent Female	Category Description
Factor 1					
Logan's Run	53	6.8	46,894	11.4%	Action, sci-fi
Soylent Green	66	7.1	51,971	11.6%	Crime, mystery, sci-fi
The Andromeda Strain	60	7.2	30,001	9.1%	Sci-fi, thriller
The Omega Man	56	6.6	26,420	7.9%	Action, sci-fi, thriller
Westworld	77	7.0	46,137	8.8%	Action, sci-fi, thriller
Fantastic Voyage	None	6.8	15,554	8.9%	Adventure, family, sci-fi
The Land That Time Forgot	None	5.7	4,915	8.0%	Adventure, fantasy
Factor 2					
Psycho	97	8.5	527,957	19.9%	Horror, mystery, thriller

The Bride of Frankenstein	None	7.9	38,670	13.3%	Drama, horror, sci-fi
Rosemary's Baby	96	8.0	167,461	22.2%	Drama, horror
The Fly	None	7.1	18,606	12.4%	Drama, horror, sci-fi
King Kong	90	7.9	72,981	11.2%	Adventure, horror, sci-fi
Invasion of the Body Snatchers	92	7.8	40,170	12.5%	Drama, horror, sci-fi
Factor 3					
20,000 Leagues Under the Sea	None	7.2	25,758	10.1%	Adventure, drama, family
Forbidden Planet	None	7.6	40,722	8.8%	Action, adventure, sci-fi
The Wizard of Oz	100	8.0	348,129	26.7%	Adventure, family, fantasy
The Day the Earth Stood Still	None	7.8	71,638	11.0%	Drama, sci-fi

In an earlier study, I reported data about a different set of science fiction movies from the highly respected MovieLens database.[22] It accurately describes itself as the primary academic center for movie-related recommender system research:

> MovieLens is a research site run by GroupLens Research at the University of Minnesota. MovieLens uses "collaborative filtering" technology to make recommendations of movies that you might enjoy, and to help you avoid the ones that you won't. Based on your movie ratings, MovieLens generates personalized predictions for movies you haven't seen yet. MovieLens is a unique research vehicle for dozens of undergraduates and graduate students researching various aspects of personalization and filtering technologies.[23]

---

[22]   Bainbridge, W.S., 2020. *The Social Structure of Online Communities* (Cambridge, England: Cambridge University Press).

[23]   movielens.org/info/about

The heart of the system is asking the user to rate some movies, then recommending others that tended to correlate in the ratings by earlier users, but it is not limited to that correlational approach, allowing users to specify movie genres, release dates, actors, and directors, and increasingly other variables.[24] If scholars in the humanities and social scientists want to explore the potential of a convergent cultural science, they might well be advised to try doing research studies in collaboration with MovieLens.

Several of the most widely used recommender system algorithms do not perform anything like factor analysis on movie preferences across the entire dataset, but take each respondent, hunt for the *neighborhood* of similar people, and use only their data to make the recommendations.[25] To conclude this section, however, one more correlational analysis will help make useful points, employing the Netflix "data set of 100,480,507 ratings that 480,189 users gave to 17,770 movies," shared in 2006 with the public in a contest to see who could develop algorithms better than those already in use.[26] Table 2.3 shows results of statistical analysis of six of the movies, the four from factor 1 with the highest number of pageviews, and the one with the most pageviews from each of the other two factors. The diagonal, from upper left, shows the number who rated each film, for example, 14,384 rating *Logan's Run* on a 1 to 5 scale. The cells below and

[24] Harper, F.M., and J.A. Konstan. 2015. "The MovieLens Datasets: History and Context." *ACM Transactions on Interactive Intelligent Systems*, files.grouplens.org/papers/harper-tiis2015.pdf

[25] Resnick, P., N. Iacovou, M. Suchak, P. Bergstrom, and J. Riedl. 1994. "GroupLens: An Open Architecture for Collaborative Filtering of Netnews." In *Proceedings of the 1994 ACM Conference on Computer Supported Cooperative Work, CSCW '94*, 175–186. New York, NY: ACM; Hill, W., L. Stead, M. Rosenstein, and G. Furnas. 1995. "Recommending and Evaluating Choices in a Virtual Community of Use." In *Proceedings of the SIGCHI Conference on Human Factors in Computing Systems, CHI '95*, 194–201. New York, NY: ACM; Sarwar, B., G. Karypis, J. Konstan, and J. Riedl. 2001. "Item-based Collaborative Filtering Recommendation Algorithms." In *Proceedings of the 10th International Conference on World Wide Web*, WWW '01, 285–295, New York, NY: ACM; Herlocker, J., J.A. Konstan, and J. Riedl. 2002. "An Empirical Analysis of Design Choices in Neighborhood-Based Collaborative Filtering Algorithms." *Information Retrieval* 5, no. 4, pp. 287–310.

[26] en.wikipedia.org/wiki/Netflix_Prize

Table 2.3 Comparative analysis using the 2006 Netflix movie database

	Logan	Soylent	Omega	Westworld	Psycho	Wizard
Logan's Run	14,384	0.43	0.42	0.39	0.17	0.17
Soylent Green	4,977	11,276	0.50	0.41	0.22	0.16
The Omega Man	3,122	3,309	5,736	0.40	0.16	0.16
Westworld	4,447	3,751	2,641	8,239	0.21	0.18
Psycho	7,651	5,930	3,225	4,856	58,837	0.26
The Wizard of Oz	8,556	6,131	3,218	5,023	31,409	74,829

to the left give the number who rated each pair, 4,977 in the combination of *Logan's Run* and *Soylent Green*. The numbers above and to the right are the correlation coefficients, in this case 0.43 which indicates that respondents who liked *Logan's Run* rather strongly also tended to like *Soylent Green*. The total number of respondents rating any of these movies was 110,465. Just 956 rated all 6, while 69,246 rated only 1 and thus could not be used in the correlation analysis.

The most obvious pattern in the table is that the four movies from factor 1 tend to correlate well and about equally with each other, replicating the analysis done with data more than a quarter century older. This suggests that the structure of movie culture is somewhat stable over time, at least in some sectors. The 0.50 correlation between *Soylent Green* and *The Omega Man* is noticeably higher than the others, probably because audiences recognized the same lead actor in both, but perhaps also for stylistic commonalities shaped by the fact this pair had the same producer. The correlations between the factor 1 quartet and the two other movies are much lower, and we see a moderate but respectable correlation of 0.26 between *Psycho* and *The Wizard of Oz*, perhaps reflecting the fact that they were both of older vintage than the quartet. Given that people vary in how much they like movies in general, and positive response biases are often found in questionnaire data, the three 0.16 coefficients may not really be meaningfully more than zero. But the differences across the coefficients are significant and indicate that commercial recommender system data can indeed be used to map cultural structures.

Audience-Generated Culture

To gain a sense of the variety of recommender systems that already exist and to raise more methodological challenges and opportunities, we shall now examine the case of The Foundry, a software system incorporated in the massively multiplayer online game *Neverwinter* that allowed players to create their own virtual environments and missions for other players to undertake. This is an excellent example for cultural science, because *Neverwinter* is one component of the vast *Dungeons and Dragons* subculture that nicely illustrates the convergence–divergence dynamic, having drawn into itself elements of many existing subcultures, then greatly stimulating the emergence of new subcultures. In a recent chapter about online virtual worlds, I reported[27]:

> A revolutionary development was the emergence of *Dungeons and Dragons* (D&D) in 1974, a tabletop role-playing game that allowed players to invent their own stories or follow an increasing number of partially prewritten scripts, usually within a fantasy environment that was frankly influenced by *Lord of the Rings*, but avoided copyright infringement by calling Hobbits *halflings* instead.[28] Another one of the many influences was *jetan*, a chesslike game devised by Edgar Rice Burroughs for *Chessmen of Mars*, one of a series of novels that also influenced the *Star Wars* mythos and that embedded the gameplay in the fictional history of competing alien ethnicities.[29]

The freedom to create their own missions, or use role-play stories written by professionals, was central to D&D culture. Thus, it was natural for Cryptic Studios to include that feature when it released *Neverwinter* in 2013. It had included similar features in two earlier online multiplayer

---

[27] Bainbridge, W.S. 2019. *Virtual Local Manufacturing Communities: Online Simulations of Future Workshop Systems*, 31. New York, NY: Business Expert Press.

[28] Gygax, G. 1979. *Advanced Dungeons and Dragons, Dungeon Masters Guide*. New York, NY: TSR/Random House.

[29] Burroughs, E.R. 1922. *Chessmen of Mars*. Chicago: A.C. McClurg.

games, *City of Heroes*, which shut down in 2012, and *Star Trek Online*, where I had studied The Foundry extensively.[30] On March 4, 2019, Cryptic announced that The Foundry would be removed from both of the surviving virtual worlds on April 11.[31] I had done some research on *Neverwinter's* version of The Foundry and, given how fundamental play-er-created material was to D&D culture, I immediately rushed to collect as much additional data as I could, especially the public recommender system data concerning more than a thousand missions. This makes the point that many forms of culture, even important ones, are ephemeral and thus require active documentation and archiving by researchers.[32]

When looking for a mission to undertake, players could open a cat-alog interface and conduct a search, for example, checking the popular missions that had received the highest ratings from earlier players or nar-rowing the search to a particular language and specifying a keyword that should be in the description written by the creator of the mission. Some missions were simple and brief, but others took as much as an hour. At the end, the player got the opportunity to rate the mission on a scale from 1 to 5 "stars," write a brief comment, and then respond to a 13-item questionnaire that listed features that any mission might have. For exam-ple, one item was "story focus," and the player could check a box if the mission seemed to have a strong narrative. Another choice was "combat focus," and the player could select either, both, or neither. A player who performed the mission a second time could update this personal evalu-ation, but would be counted only once for the rating and classification. Many players who assigned a rating declined to offer any categorization, and it is common for recommender systems to collect more fragmentary data than do social science questionnaires. Table 2.4 reports the distribu-tion of classifications for all the missions in the public database, for the six languages other than English.

---

[30]   Bainbridge, W.S. 2016. *Star Worlds: Freedom Versus Control in Online Game-worlds*. Ann Arbor, Michigan: University of Michigan Press.

[31]   Kael, A. March 4, 2019. "Foundry Sunset—April 11, 2019." www.arcgames.com/en/games/neverwinter/news/detail/11102923

[32]   forums.mmorpg.com/discussion/480490/whats-the-future-of-player-made-content-in-the-mmorpg-genre

Table 2.4 Player categorizations of player-created game missions

	German	French	Polish	Portuguese	Italian	Turkish
Challeng-ing	12.1%	5.2%	9.7%	23.5%	11.7%	12.3%
Story focus	10.4%	14.0%	10.7%	7.8%	10.1%	12.4%
Combat focus	16.0%	12.7%	18.9%	12.8%	9.5%	16.0%
Lore	2.3%	1.1%	6.5%	5.8%	3.2%	4.1%
Exploration	8.3%	8.0%	3.8%	9.6%	6.6%	7.8%
Humor	7.1%	8.7%	9.7%	9.3%	9.6%	8.1%
Unusual	5.7%	7.0%	7.2%	7.8%	6.4%	7.9%
Solo friendly	17.5%	21.4%	10.3%	4.6%	15.9%	3.7%
Group friendly	3.0%	3.3%	3.7%	2.7%	5.1%	3.8%
Role-play	4.7%	5.8%	4.4%	2.5%	3.5%	4.9%
Puzzle	2.1%	2.2%	2.0%	2.2%	2.8%	3.1%
Adjustable difficulty	1.7%	2.5%	3.0%	5.0%	4.4%	4.3%
Eventful	9.1%	8.1%	9.9%	6.5%	11.0%	11.5%
	100.0%	100.0%	100.0%	100.0%	100.0%	100.0%
Categoriza-tions	195,505	192,438	124,098	98,645	49,710	26,333
Missions	387	313	109	217	128	79
Plays	1,091,905	774,614	505,449	434,726	345,084	201,789

There were 387 missions in the German language that had been played a total of 1,091,905 times. Among the details not shown in the table are that there were 518,338 ratings on the 1 to 5 scale, with a mean of 3.68 stars. We do not know whether only about half of the plays produced ratings simply because the players tended to do the mission twice, getting credit only for once, or that some fraction of those who completed a mission chose not to rate it. But there is a major discrepancy between the 518,338 ratings and the 195,505 categorizations. If one player marked both questionnaire boxes for story focused and combat focused, that would count as one rating and two categorizations. We just do not know how many categorizations the average categorizer gave, but it appears that only a small fraction of the players went this far in the recommendation process. This complex situation offers two insights:

1. Participants in a culture differ in their knowledge of it and in their willingness to share observations or assessments.
2. In cultural science, the nature of the "unit of analysis" is often optional.

As I defined the term in an earlier textbook-software educational project, a unit of analysis is "the thing being counted or the basic element of reality that constitutes a case of the thing being studied."[33] The unit of analysis in questionnaire survey research is typically the individual respondent. This makes particular sense in political science election polling, because each voter gets one vote. But in culture, some individuals may be far more influential than others, and for decades social scientists have distinguished *opinion leaders* from the rank and file members of the population.[34] In Table 2.4 the unit of analysis is the assignment of a mission to a category by one player who may have assigned it as well to other categories, each assignment counting separately.

The 13 category names in Table 2.4 are all the information The Foundry gave its users about the meanings of these terms. Any player would understand the distinction between "solo friendly" and "group friendly," but the exact meanings are open to debate. "Solo friendly" states clearly that it is possible for a single player to complete the mission without help from other players. "Group friendly" does not explicitly state that a team of players is necessary, and for many missions additional players could be a hindrance rather than a help. An alternate definition is that a group-friendly mission is one that a group of friends would have fun completing, even if one of them could easily have "soloed" it. It is worth noting that solo categorizations were far more common than group categorizations, and a constant debate about online role-playing games is whether they implicitly discourage group play, even as they seek to be

---

[33]   Bainbridge, W.S. 1989. *Survey Research: A Computer-Assisted Introduction*, 366. Belmont, California: Wadsworth.

[34]   Katz, E., and P. Lazarsfeld. 1955. *Personal Influence*. New York, NY: Free Press.

multiplayer. The low numbers for the "lore" category are also interesting, because we might have predicted that D&D fans would have prioritized the mythos, for example, the fact that *Neverwinter* is the name of a city governed by Lord Protector Dagult Neverember, within the Forgotten Realms part of the D&D backstory.[35]

Whatever language is supposedly spoken in the fictional city of Neverwinter, the *Neverwinter* game was created in English, and then translated to German, French, Polish, Portuguese, Italian, and Turkish. The novels of the popular American D&D author R.A. Salvatore have been translated into German, Italian, Finnish, Hebrew, Greek, Hungarian, Turkish, Croatian, Bulgarian, Yiddish, Spanish, Russian, Polish, Czech, and French.[36] Cryptic Studios is currently owned by a Chinese company with the imposing name Perfect World Entertainment.[37] So we are clearly examining a cross-cultural subculture, and it is an open question whether there are cultural differences across the six language cultures represented in Table 2.4. I often thought about this issue as I entered the data into my computer, because the only way to extract this information from the software for this particular game was to do so manually, working from "screenshot" pictures of the game display. The data raise this question, but they do not answer it.

Massively multiplayer online games are primarily produced in the United States, China, and South Korea, with some production in Britain and Germany, and a few highly creative game studios in such places as Iceland and Norway. Poland has recently entered the game industry, notably with the impressive and popular *Witcher* series of fantasy games.[38] Spanish is missing from the list of *Neverwinter* Foundry missions, although I did find a couple of Spanish language missions hidden in the English category. In 2013, soon after *Neverwinter's* release, several Spanish-speakers complained online, including someone using the moniker SpellSigner in the online forums of the Steam game distributor: "Es ridiculo esto. El juego está hasta en Turco y Portugués, pero del español no habla ni 2 palabras."

---

[35] forgottenrealms.fandom.com/wiki/Neverwinter

[36] forgottenrealms.fandom.com/wiki/R.A._Salvatore

[37] en.wikipedia.org/wiki/Cryptic_Studios

[38] en.wikipedia.org/wiki/The_Witcher_(video_game)

Cat Hugger replied, "Or you could just learn English and this way be able to enjoy thousands of other english only-games. Just a thought!"[39]

The inclusion of Portuguese in the list reflects the population of Brazil more than Portugal, and the popular scripting language used with many games, Lua, was developed there.[40] We cannot definitively interpret the two obvious statistical facts about the Portuguese data in Table 2.4, that Portuguese missions are more challenging and that Portuguese speakers produce twice as many missions as the French, despite similar numbers of plays. The reason relates to the issue of unit of analysis, because a few players produced many short-duration missions in Portuguese, and the demise of The Foundry prevents us from playing all of the missions to see how they were designed.

Here we shift the definition of unit of analysis from the categorization to the mission, conceptually jumping right over the player. In social science, it is quite common to perform statistical analysis of data originally concerning individual people, but aggregated by geographic area. Having often done statistical research of that kind, I am very aware of the problems of defining geographic units. For example, much American government data can be analyzed by *metropolitan statistical areas*, which traditionally matched county boundaries except in New England, and some of the "units" seemed heterogeneous, notably the Baltimore–Washington metropolitan area, given how different the city of Baltimore is from the nation's capital. Foundry mission creators differed in whether they would break a very long mission into parts, each of which would then count as a separate mission. In Foundry data, we cannot be sure which missions are copies or adaptations of others. Also, the recommender system featured specific missions for a few days and reports data from that period separately from data for other periods for the same mission, leaving open the question of whether they should be combined. Here I simply accept the unit of analysis as reported in *Neverwinter*, but focus on cases that meet reasonable criteria to maximize the meaningfulness of the data.

First, we will focus just on missions that took players on average at least 10 minutes to complete. The Foundry database reported average

---

[39]   steamcommunity.com/app/109600/discussions/0/648813727946039645/
[40]   en.wikipedia.org/wiki/Lua_(programming_language)

duration for all missions that meet this criterion, but did not report the durations of shorter missions. Of the total 1,233 missions in Table 2.3, 649 of them took on average 10 minutes or more to complete. Multiplying their specific average duration by the numbers of plays gives the remarkable total of 612,764 hours! This does not include the time invested by players who did not complete a mission, nor the times for the missions under 10 minutes. The reason for excluding the short missions is that many of them were not missions at all, but quick in-out actions, such as saying hello to a computer-simulated person to earn a simulated white pearl.

Second, we focus on missions that received at least 100 ratings on the star scale of quality. Another option would have been to focus just on missions that received 100 categorizations, or some other number. However, that alternative might distort the balance between very specialized missions that had their votes concentrated in one category versus those that were more general and got many votes from each rater. The English language missions were also included, giving a total of 774 missions with durations of at least 10 minutes and having at least 100 star quality votes. This will allow us to correlate categorizations, using mission as the unit of analysis. However, there are multiple ways to handle correlations in a situation like this, and Table 2.5 reports the results of two of them, focusing just on the eight categories with clear cultural significance.

Table 2.5 The correlation structure of game mission descriptors

	Story	Combat	Lore	Explore	Humor	Un-usual	Role-play	Puzzle
Story	1.00	−0.65	0.35	0.32	0.04	−0.05	0.69	−0.03
Combat	0.56	1.00	-0.35	−0.48	−0.30	−0.39	−0.53	−0.44
Lore	0.88	0.55	1.00	0.05	−0.07	0.00	0.26	0.19
Exploration	0.88	0.59	0.81	1.00	−0.23	−0.01	0.29	0.36
Humor	0.63	0.50	0.44	0.45	1.00	0.46	−0.02	−0.06
Unusual	0.85	0.57	0.64	0.75	0.79	1.00	0.01	0.29
Role-play	0.89	0.54	0.88	0.81	0.49	0.62	1.00	−0.01
Puzzle	0.63	0.45	0.60	0.79	0.36	0.58	0.61	1.00

The diagonal of cells in the table from upper left to lower right simply reports that each variable has a Pearson correlation coefficient of 1.00 with itself. The coefficients below and to the left of the diagonal are the results of correlating the raw numbers. They are rather large, as questionnaire correlations usually go, simply because they reflect the overall number of categorization votes each mission received, and some missions had been played and classified by far more players than others. It is interesting that the 0.56 correlation between story focus and combat focus is far less than the other correlations in the story focus column, but it is hard to know exactly what this means prior to completing the alternate analysis.

The correlations above and to the right of the diagonal are much easier to interpret. Before calculating them, the data for each mission were transformed into what fraction of the total number of categorizations for a given mission was assigned to the particular category. While not perfect, this is a pretty good method for removing the distorting effect of the highly varied number of categorizations across missions. Here we see a very strong negative correlation of -0.65 between story focus and combat focus, indicating that these characteristics are rather contradictory. Looking across the top row we see that story focus has solid positive correlations with lore (0.35), exploration (0.32), and role-play (0.69). Looking over the whole table we see a connection of 0.46 between humor and unusual, and 0.36 between exploration and puzzle. Frankly, this method allows the data to speak very clearly, helping us understand the meanings of the categories and how they fit together.

Although The Foundry no longer exists, many other online systems support creativity by members of the audience for popular culture franchises and folk traditions. Recently, vast numbers of nonprofessional writers have published their stories online, notably in the *fan fiction* context. Among the most popular is the *Star Wars* subculture, commercially manifested in many media, including computer games, novels, television programs, and most centrally, three trilogies of movies, the last of which was not yet complete at the time of this writing. As of May 5, 2019, Archive of Our Own offered online access to fully 4,775,000 stories and other works, including 87,412 directly inspired by *Star Wars*. It defines itself as "A fan-created, fan-run, nonprofit, noncommercial archive for

Table 2.6 Co-occurrence of characters in fan fiction stories

	Obi	Luke	Han	Leia	Anakin	Padmé	Rey	Finn
Obi-Wan Kenobi	12,134	17.4%	10.6%	10.3%	73.3%	64.4%	2.8%	2.8%
Luke Sky-walker	16.8%	11,720	55.7%	47.0%	17.2%	25.1%	22.3%	22.8%
Han Solo	7.9%	42.7%	8,995	45.5%	8.5%	11.5%	16.1%	18.4%
Leia Organa	13.0%	61.4%	77.4%	15,303	15.1%	25.9%	34.5%	43.3%
Anakin Sky-walker	47.1%	11.5%	7.4%	7.7%	7,802	64.2%	2.4%	2.4%
Padmé Amidala	24.4%	9.8%	5.9%	7.8%	37.8%	4,592	1.8%	1.7%
Rey	4.5%	37.2%	35.2%	44.1%	6.1%	7.6%	19,595	74.7%
Finn	3.0%	25.4%	26.7%	36.8%	4.0%	4.9%	49.7%	13,037

transformative fanworks, like fanfiction, fanart, fan videos, and podfic."[41] The archive's search engine facilitates identification of many interesting subsets, such as all the stories that contain a specified pair of familiar *Star Wars* characters, including the eight reported in Table 2.6.

Each column of the table reports the number of stories that include the character named at the top, on the row that has that same name, and the percentage co-appearance with characters named on the other rows. Of the 87,412 works related to *Star Wars*, 12,134 included the character Obi-Wan Kenobi, who was a somewhat elderly Jedi master when he mentored Luke Skywalker in the original 1977 movie. Of the stories including him, 2,038 (16.8 percent) also included Luke, but rather more, 5,719 (47.1 percent), included Anakin Skywalker. The explanation will be obvious to any *Star Wars* fan. The second trilogy of movies takes place earlier in the fictional history, when Obi-Wan was a young man who interacted with Anakin Skywalker, who was Luke's father, and Obi-Wan died before the end of the 1977 film. Padmé Amidala was Luke's mother, but she

---

[41] archiveofourown.org

died and he was raised as an orphan by an uncle and aunt. Rey and Finn were central characters in the third trilogy, which took place later in the history, and thus only a very unusual story could justify including them along with Anakin and Padmé.

An analysis like Table 2.6 may not contain surprises for members of the particular subculture, although it may call their attention to interesting anomalies like the stories that contain both Luke and Anakin. But it can serve as a useful introduction for students and scholars who are not members of the subculture and provide a framework to guide their further study. Professional literary critics and literature professors will still be able to express their own views after cultural science is well established, but much of their work should focus on how knowledgeable audiences interpret a subculture to which they belong. The table is like a recommender system, but based on observation of behavior, not expression of opinions in response to a questionnaire.

By writing a story that includes both Luke and Anakin, at least some of the amateur writers demonstrated that the relationship between these characters deserves consideration, and reading what they wrote may provide the material for scholarship, social-scientific analysis of family relationships, or even provide an idea for a future movie in which time travel overcomes death of a parent. Oh, wait! Anakin did not immediately die, but morphed into Darth Vader, the chief enemy of the original trilogy. The archive has 1,612 stories that contain Darth Vader, 729 of which also contain Luke; 346 contain Anakin, and 184 contain all three personalities. We can imagine a journal article based on deep analysis of these 184 works. Table 2.6 would only be the first step toward a serious cultural science analysis, whether a monograph or collection of essays written by a diversity of authors, or even a complex computer game in which the player could choose not only which character to become, but which others would appear as artificially intelligent nonplayer characters.

Conclusion

Although the fact is seldom noted, here we saw that recommender systems are rather similar to the questionnaire research developed long ago in sociology and political science, and thus may offer solutions to the serious problems faced by that traditional methodology today. Two related problems deserve mention: (1) response rates have dropped rather low in questionnaire research, failing to achieve representative samples, and (2) many kinds of questionnaire items have very different meanings for the culturally diverse population, thus obscuring the implication of statistical results. Similar problems plague ethnography and related forms of field observation in the social sciences. Originally, cultural anthropology tended to assume that each "primitive" society had a relatively coherent and uniform culture, and so elaborate population sampling methods were not necessary, but if that was ever true in the past, it is not true today. Thus, while social science can contribute to the convergence of the humanities with information science, it also needs help from these partner disciplines.

CHAPTER 3

Modernizing Questionnaire Survey Research and Ethnography

Traditional research methods for studying culture in the humanities and cultural anthropology were qualitative, rather than quantitative, and early anthropologists tended to assume that each distinct culture was uniform within itself and thus *ethnography* did not require statistical sampling procedures. However, for 70 years, the Human Relations Area Files at Yale University have collected quantitative data "to promote understanding of cultural diversity and commonality in the past and present."[1] The journal *World Cultures* emphasizes a related methodological approach, the analysis of "aggregate cultural data in coded form on a large sample of societies."[2] For decades, cultural anthropologists have been aware that no culture is totally uniform and that the degree of uniformity varies greatly.[3] Survey researchers may cogently argue that their methods offer both a broader and more rigorous perspective than that possessed by an ethnographic field researcher who is embedded among some of the people under study. However, in recent years, surveys have faced increasing difficulty studying systematic samples of the population, and their advantages measuring large-scale public opinion may be of limited value in studying subcultures or the realities of daily life. In addition to online questionnaires, there now are many kinds of rather systematic data, even quantitative, available for researchers, using Internet as a virtual hilltop from which to observe cultures.

---

[1] hraf.yale.edu

[2] www.worldcultures.org

[3] Edgerton, R.B. 1966. "Conceptions of Psychosis in Four East African Societies." *American Anthropologist* 2, no. 1, pp. 408–425.

Variations on the Theme of Musicology

Since 1972, the General Social Survey (GSS) has been a mainstay of sociological research, although its character changed somewhat as it matured, and only briefly did it collect data about music. Originally, it could be described as a tool of the Social Indicator movement that wanted to maximize the benefit of U.S. government programs and policies, and therefore needed a reliable way to assess the condition of the general population. In so doing it would supplement surveys by the Census Bureau and engage academics in the debates about where social life in America was going. To accomplish this, it would periodically send interviewers to the homes of a cluster sample of Americans to ask the same questions to see if the answers were changing, such as "Last week were you working full time, part time, going to school, keeping house, or what?" In 1972 this question was asked of 1,613 respondents, and by 2016 the total over the years had reached 62,447. "Keeping house" had dropped from 26.8 percent to 9.9 percent, reflecting the gradual entry of more women into the workforce.

All the GSS data are available online for anybody to analyze, at the Survey Documentation and Analysis (SDA) website:

> SDA is a set of programs for the documentation and Web-based analysis of survey data. SDA was developed, distributed and supported by the Computer-assisted Survey Methods Program (CSM) at the University of California, Berkeley until the end of 2014. Beginning in 2015, CSM is managed and supported by the Institute for Scientific Analysis, a private, non-profit organization, under an exclusive continuing license agreement with the University of California.[4]

In 1995 I was honored to manage the initial funding through National Science Foundation grant 9422785:

---

[4] sda.berkeley.edu/index.html

This is a prototype Internet service for the General Social Survey employing NCSA Mosaic. The project will develop a system to provide enhanced access to survey data, using the General Social Survey for implementation of these integrated services, which will subsequently be extended to a variety of other survey data sets. These services will provide facilities for hypertext viewing and searching of complete survey documentation, customized and documented extracts from data sets, statistical analysis, and File Transfer Protocol delivery of full or extracted data sets. The General Social Survey is an ideal source of survey material to develop the system, because it is a highly diverse large dataset of complex structure, extensively documented in terms of publications based on each item, and has already been the basis of more than three thousand scientific publications and dissertations.[5]

NCSA Mosaic was the first widely available web browser, and this project was a pilot study on how the web could be used for educational purposes and as an active archive for scientists and scholars.

The Social Indicator movement was somewhat controversial, because significant fractions of the public and the political world were opposed to government social activism, but it also turned out that social scientists wanted the GSS to ask many new kinds of questions that they could analyze for academic publications. Therefore, the GSS began adding topical modules in addition to a somewhat limited set of constant social indicators. In 1993, the GSS included a culture module with a section measuring preference for styles of music that can illustrate some of the factors that shape cultural science. The GSS asked respondents to rate each of 18 genres of music on this scale from 1 to 5: dislike it very much, dislike it, mixed feelings, like it, or like it very much. Table 3.1 reports correlations among eight of these genres, selected because their structure offers generalizable insights. The correlation coefficients are tau-b, in which an item correlates 1.00 with itself and 0.00 with another genre with which it has absolutely no relationship, and has negative correlations if liking

---

[5]   www.nsf.gov/awardsearch/showAward?AWD_ID=9422785

Table 3.1 Preference correlations among music genres

	Classical	Opera	Broad-way	Jazz	New Age	Gospel	Rock	Metal
Classical	1.00	0.50	0.40	0.23	0.17	0.04	0.02	–0.01
Opera	0.50	1.00	0.38	0.20	0.17	0.09	–0.01	0.01
Broad-way	0.40	0.38	1.00	0.22	0.08	0.08	0.05	–0.10
Jazz	0.23	0.20	0.22	1.00	0.25	0.02	0.22	0.10
New Age	0.17	0.17	0.08	0.25	1.00	–0.12	0.26	0.34
Gospel	0.04	0.09	0.08	0.02	–0.12	1.00	–0.17	–0.18
Rock	0.02	–0.01	0.05	0.22	0.26	–0.17	1.00	0.32
Metal	–0.01	0.01	–0.10	0.10	0.34	–0.18	0.32	1.00
Like it	49.6%	21.9%	52.6%	51.1%	18.0%	59.5%	55.1%	11.2%
Answered	1,529	1,510	1,515	1,553	1,300	1,559	1,544	1,526

one genre implies hating the other. The rows and columns of the table are arranged in terms of the correlations with classical music.

Not surprisingly, there is a strong 0.50 correlation between liking classical music and liking opera. However, they are not equally popular, 49.6 percent of the respondents saying they liked classical music, compared with only 21.9 percent who like opera, combining the "like" and "like very much" responses. Broadway musicals are American, rather than European as in the case of most classical music, but drew upon the classical tradition. Classical music has essentially no correlations with gospel, contemporary rock, or heavy metal music, which have their own distinctive correlation patterns. While 1,529 respondents answered the question about liking classical music, only 1,300 answered the one about New Age, probably because some respondents were not familiar with it. Those who did respond gave it rather low ratings, only 18.0 percent liking it, while it correlated moderately with both contemporary rock, which got a favorable 55.1 percent preference score, and heavy metal, which was least popular at 11.2 percent.

The most popular musical genre in this set of eight, liked by 59.5 percent of the respondents, was gospel music. It lacks strong positive correlations, but has negative correlations with new age, contemporary rock, and heavy metal. Here we encounter again one of the most difficult problems in the analysis of preference data. Respondents may vary in terms of response bias, some tending to give favorable ratings and others giving more unfavorable ratings, which would have the effect of inflating positive correlations and deflating negative ones. Among the many ways cultural science can deal with response bias is to consider other items as well. For example, a standard GSS item asks "How often do you attend religious services?" Of the 250 respondents who never attend religious services, 44.4 percent like gospel music, compared with 84.4 percent of the 135 who attend more than once a week. Of those who never attend religious services, 19.8 percent like heavy metal, compared with only 3.1 percent of the most frequent attenders. The example is a good one, because it is easy to comprehend in cultural terms. Obviously, gospel music is connected to traditional religion, while heavy metal is secular.

A second general observation is that the traditional plan of administering a questionnaire or interview to a statistically representative random sample of the general population may be too costly but also not necessary, if the goal is to explore cultural differences. The current NSF grant supporting the GSS cost fully $15,726,165.[6] This has supported two main GSS surveys, four GSS components of the International Social Survey Program, plus "designing an extensive, rigorous experiment comparing an Internet GSS survey to the standard GSS." Already in 2001, Tom W. Smith, the GSS leader, reported the results of comparing Internet-based and in-person surveys, finding somewhat limited differences in his particular dataset.[7] By 2014 he was advocating a multilevel, multisource (ML-MS) approach to improving survey research, at one point commenting:

> Human societies are complex, multi-faceted entities and social-science research designs need to measure that complexity. A key requirement is contextualization. Most people live in households which are nested in neighborhoods, communities, and countries.

---

[6]   www.nsf.gov/awardsearch/showAward?AWD_ID=1458922

[7]   Smith, T.W. 2001. "An Experimental Comparison of Internet and In-Person Surveys." *National Opinion Research Center*, gss.norc.org/Documents/reports/methodological-reports/MR095.pdf

They are not isolated individuals, but interact with and are notably influenced by their families, neighborhoods, communities, nations, etc. Surveys need to collect information on each of these levels from the individual to the nation so the contexts in which people live are understood and that through multi-level analysis the impacts of these different levels can be measured and modeled.[8]

In 1998 I joined the team led by James Witte that deployed two vast online studies, Survey2000 and Survey2001, to explore issues of how well online respondents represented the general population.[9] In 2002 I published an exploration of this difficult topic, using a subset of the data based on responses from children aged 13 to 15.[10] The main finding was that often, if not always, subsamples with different biases may show roughly the same correlations between variables. Of course, members of a well-organized subculture may exhibit much finer distinctions between elements of their own culture than do outsiders, which implies that cultural scientists may often decide to use purposive samples rather than random samples. The early-teenage data offered a first step toward this methodology because the respondents had been recruited in different ways. Of 2,942 respondents aged 13 to 15, 51.3 percent completed the questionnaire at home, largely recruited voluntarily through the National Geographic websites, while 40.6 percent did so at school, mostly in an assignment that National Geographic had organized at two schools in

---

[8]   Smith, T.W., and J. Kim. 2014. "The Multi-Level, Multi-Source (ML-MS) Approach to Improving Survey Research." *GSS Methodological Report*, 121, National Opinion Research Center.

[9]   Witte, J.C., L.M. Amoroso, and P.E.N. Howard. 2000. "Method and Representation in Internet-Based Survey Tools: Mobility, Community, and Cultural Identity in Survey 2000." *Social Science Computer Review* 18, no. 2, pp. 179–195; Pargas, R.P., J.C. Witte, K. Jaganathan, and J.S. Davis. 2003. "Database Design for Dynamic Online Surveys." In *Proceedings of the Conference on Information Technology: Coding and Computing*, 665–671, Las Vegas, Nevada: IEEE.

[10]   Bainbridge, W.S. 2002. "Validity of Web-Based Surveys." In *Computing in the Social Sciences and Humanities*, eds. O.V. Burton, 51–66. Urbana, Illinois: University of Illinois Press.

Table 3.2 Music preferences from an online survey

	Like or like very much		Correlation with female	
	Home	**School**	**Home**	**School**
Classic, symphony, and chamber music	51.7%	23.4%	0.08	0.02
Opera	14.4%	7.8%	0.12	0.00
Broadway musicals/show tunes	46.5%	29.1%	0.29	0.20
Jazz	45.8%	33.1%	0.00	−0.04
Big band/swing	50.0%	42.7%	0.09	0.03
Mood/easy listening	37.6%	26.5%	0.09	0.09
Country and western	17.6%	18.4%	0.11	0.06
Bluegrass	10.3%	9.5%	0.05	−0.11
Hymns/gospel	26.1%	20.1%	0.12	0.08
Rhythm and blues	41.3%	33.8%	−0.01	−0.02
Rap/hip-hop	41.3%	61.4%	0.07	−0.01
Dance music (e.g., electronica)	45.8%	54.2%	0.16	0.24
Caribbean (e.g., reggae, soca, calypso)	38.7%	31.1%	−0.02	−0.03
Latin (e.g., mariachi, salsa)	23.2%	17.0%	0.06	0.06
Music of ethnic/national tradition	38.2%	27.9%	0.07	0.07
Modern folk/singer-songwriter	28.2%	16.3%	0.17	0.07
Contemporary pop/rock	67.1%	53.7%	0.07	0.15
Alternative rock	65.2%	61.7%	0.06	0.01
Oldies/classic rock	54.5%	38.2%	0.12	0.09
Heavy metal	25.2%	37.2%	−0.08	−0.18

each U.S. state and Canadian province. Table 3.2 reports results for music preferences, comparing these two very different samples.

The first four music genres are listed in the same order as in Table 3.1, starting with classical music that is vastly more popular among children who responded at home rather than in school. Two decades ago, when these data were collected, prosperous and well-educated households were much more likely to have good Internet connectivity, but even today we might expect big social class differences in the orientation of families toward elite or classical artistic culture. Going down the list of 20 genres, only 4 show significantly greater popularity among the children responding through the computers at their schools: rap/hip-hop, dance music (e.g., electronica), alternative rock, and heavy metal. Country and western music is about equally popular. However, as in the case of New Age mentioned earlier, some genres are not universally familiar. While there are variations between the two sets of respondents in the gender difference in a genre's popularity, it is noteworthy that the two clearest cases of female preference, Broadway musicals/show tunes and dance music (e.g., electronica), were preferred differently by the home versus school respondents.

The higher ratings for several genres among children who responded online at home may reflect Richard A. Peterson's *omnivore theory*. He proposed that people vary in the diversity of their cultural tastes, some being *omnivores* who like many different styles, and others being *univores* whose interests are very tightly focused.[11] In connection with Witte's research team, Peterson wrote an article collaborating with John Ryan about how music preferences might be evolving, given the ease of downloading it from Internet, perhaps rendering everybody omnivores. In their introduction, they noted that musical culture has already undergone a major transformation:

> As recently as two centuries ago, all popular music was embodied. The medium of transmission was the human voice as well as the breath or hand on the instrument. Transmission and reception were face-to-face and full of potential for intimacy and interactivity. Music was "live" and disappeared as soon as it was performed. The only way in which to hear music was to attend when and where a performance was taking place, and so most people knew practically nothing about other people's music.[12]

---

[11]   van Eijck, K. 2000. "Richard A. Peterson and the Culture of Consumption." *Poetics* 28, no. 2, pp. 207–224.

[12]   Peterson, R.A., and J. Ryan. 2004. "The Disembodied Muse: Music in the Internet Age." In *Society Online*, eds. P.N. Howard and S. Jones, 223. Thousand Oaks, California: Sage.

From that perspective, by allowing everybody to listen to all kinds of music, Internet may be erasing the cultural boundaries between musical genres and ethnic traditions. Conceivably, the only categories that would still be meaningful would be the personality variables of the individual members of the audience, for example, extraverted versus introverted music, and some recent research has begun to explore movie preferences in terms of the personality of the viewer.[13] While I am not convinced by that argument, it can be tested through future online surveys, and the ethnographic research technique can be conceptualized as a form of intellectual individualism.

The term *survey research* is often used as a synonym for *questionnaire research*, and yet the term *survey* can refer to systematic observation in the natural world, not just asking questions. At many online services, people engage in public behavior following systematic procedures, analogous to but possibly more genuine than a verbal response to a researcher's question. Among the clearest examples are several web-based services designed for musicians to share recordings, perhaps sell them directly online to listeners, and advertise themselves for local performance gigs. Here we will briefly look at data from Bandcamp and ReverbNation, but others include Sonicbids, Spotify, and Soundcloud.[14]

The motto at the top of Bandcamp's website urges: "Discover amazing new music and directly support the artists who make it."[15] As Wikipedia reports,

> Artists and labels upload music to Bandcamp and control how they sell it, setting their own prices, offering fans the option to pay more (which they do 40% of the time) and selling merchandise...

---

[13] Karumur, R.P., T.T. Nguyen, and J.A. Konstan. 2016. "Exploring the Value of Personality in Predicting Rating Behaviors: A Study of Category Preferences on MovieLens." In *Proceedings of the 10th ACM Conference on Recommender Systems*, 139–142. New York, NY: ACM; Karumur, R.P., T.T. Nguyen, and J.A. Konstan. 2018. "Personality, User Preferences and Behavior in Recommender Systems." *Information Systems Frontiers* 20, no. 6, pp. 1241–1265.

[14] www.sonicbids.com; www.spotify.com; soundcloud.com

[15] bandcamp.com

Table 3.3 Bandcamp music listings, showing regional cultural variations

	Classical	Devo-tional	Folk	Jazz	Rock	Electronic	Total N
Berlin	3.2%	3.3%	9.2%	10.3%	25.1%	49.0%	3,255
London	3.0%	3.0%	13.9%	9.0%	33.1%	38.0%	3,170
Vancouver	1.7%	2.6%	16.6%	4.8%	39.0%	35.3%	3,016
Sydney	1.7%	2.1%	9.8%	9.0%	33.7%	43.6%	2,478
Madrid	2.3%	2.1%	5.8%	4.1%	53.6%	32.1%	2,104
Manchester	1.1%	2.2%	9.9%	4.2%	24.2%	58.4%	1,662
Dublin	2.0%	1.2%	15.8%	4.6%	28.7%	47.7%	989
Buenos Aires	0.4%	2.0%	9.2%	2.9%	79.1%	6.4%	762
Glasgow	1.5%	0.9%	16.3%	3.4%	44.5%	33.4%	326
Amsterdam	1.2%	1.2%	8.1%	17.1%	26.7%	45.7%	322
Mexico City	1.9%	0.0%	5.6%	2.3%	54.1%	36.1%	266

Bandcamp's website offers users access to an artist's page featuring information on the artist, social media links, merchandising links and listing the artist's available music.[16]

Bandcamp's search engine permits searching for performers by 28 genres and 25 cities where many of them perform. Table 3.3 reports May 2019 data for 6 illustrative genres in the 11 cities outside the United States.

For example, we see that about half of the 3,255 performers located in Berlin, Germany, perform electronic music, frankly a term that seems modern but is a century old and has many variants, as Wikipedia correctly reports:

Electronically produced music became prevalent in the popular domain by the 1990s, because of the advent of affordable music technology. Contemporary electronic music includes many vari-

---

eties and ranges from experimental art music to popular forms such as electronic dance music. Today, pop electronic music is most recognizable in its 4/4 form and more connected with the mainstream culture as opposed to its preceding forms which were specialized to niche markets.[17]

The table also reports that a quarter of the Berlin performers in this subset of genres work in the "American" rock tradition, and only 3.2 percent in their national Bach–Beethoven classical genre. This low percentage partly just reflects the fact that Bandcamp is primarily for solo players and small bands, but it also reflects a cultural divide within a city, and the Berlin Philharmonic Orchestra has its own elaborate website.[18]

A serious study of these online music social media would want to chart the changing statistics over time, for example, monitoring the Buenos Aires performers over the next few years to see how many of them adopted the high-tech electronic systems. Looking more deeply at the performers' individual Bandcamp pages could define what each city means by "folk music," for example, looking for possible Irish influences in Glasgow folk music, given the wide popularity of Irish dance music at the present time and western Scotland's proximity to Ireland. National data from the comparable ReverbNation website in Table 3.4 may contain clues, in the Celtic column, which indicates that this Irish–Scottish tradition has some popularity in France and Germany. Yes, in India the local folk-pop Bollywood genre is vastly more popular than anywhere else, but the Christian/gospel genre is more popular in India than in France or Germany. The orientation of these sites is primarily toward independent performers, and the ReverbNation website quotes this testimonial: "It's fair to say that much of our recent success wouldn't have happened without ReverbNation. It's exactly what every starting band needs."[19]

To be sure, each online source of data such as these will reflect a particular social organization as well as subculture, and in many fields with strong commercial aspects. But each offers links to sources of other data.

---

17 en.wikipedia.org/wiki/Electronic_music
18 www.berliner-philharmoniker.de/en/
19 www.reverbnation.com

Table 3.4 National variations in musical culture, from ReverbNation listings

	Bolly-wood/ Tolly-wood	Celtic	Christ-ian rock	Christ-ian/ gospel	Classi-cal	Coun-try	Folk	Latin	Total N
United States	0.1%	1.6%	5.4%	25.1%	3.8%	40.6%	17.8%	5.6%	14,772
Canada	0.2%	2.2%	1.5%	10.7%	7.2%	44.1%	30.5%	3.3%	1,228
United Kingdom	0.3%	2.4%	1.4%	16.0%	11.5%	24.1%	42.5%	1.9%	1,064
Australia	0.2%	2.5%	1.6%	8.0%	4.6%	44.3%	36.3%	2.5%	438
India	49.3%	0.0%	4.1%	16.2%	14.9%	6.1%	9.1%	0.3%	296
Germany	0.0%	4.8%	1.6%	6.9%	18.0%	26.5%	32.8%	9.5%	189
France	0.0%	5.9%	1.3%	5.3%	23.7%	10.5%	42.1%	11.2%	152
Italy	0.0%	2.9%	0.7%	8.8%	27.2%	14.0%	28.7%	17.6%	136
Mexico	0.0%	0.0%	4.7%	15.7%	7.9%	9.4%	11.8%	50.4%	127

For example, it would be easy to take random or purposive samples of the performers listed by Bandcamp and ReverbNation and then interview them or send them questionnaires. Perhaps the Glasgow folk music is performed on high-technology bagpipes! Oh, and intrepid researchers could also attend public performances! That raises the point that their audiences may also be worthy of study, and that in today's online world communities of fans are easy to find.

Comparative Surveys Across Subcultures

No form of culture, other than perhaps family structures, has been the focus of social scientific research more than religion. Sociologists tend to name a Frenchman, Emile Durkheim, and a German, Max Weber, as the founders of their field, although British and American schools of sociology were already in existence when those two began publishing. The 1897 book *Suicide*, by Durkheim, contrasts Protestants with Catholics in their rates of self-destruction, while Weber contrasted their differences with respect to economics in his 1904 book *The Protestant Ethic and the*

Spirit of Capitalism.[20] The U.S. government conducted censuses of religious organizations in 1890, 1906, 1916, 1926, and 1936, which more recent researchers have found very valuable for statistical analysis. Data from the four 20th-century surveys can be freely downloaded from the digital library of the Association of Religion Data Archives, in a form I contributed after Rodney Stark and I had used them in our 1996 book, *Religion, Deviance and Social Control.*[21] This dataset compiles information regarding the religious composition of 378 cities in the United States from 1906 to 1936 and contains 90 variables, including observations on church membership, growth, and suicide rates.[22]

Another dataset I contributed to ARDA was a 244-item questionnaire completed by 1,025 members of the Endtime Family, or Children of God (CoG), a religious group that is in high tension with its surrounding cultural environment. This dataset assesses the validity of applying survey data techniques to unusual religious groups. Additionally, most of the variables were taken from the GSS, enabling comparisons between the Endtime Family and the general population.[23] This illustrates a general principle of cross-cultural research: A scientific instrument developed to chart the structure of one culture can subsequently be adapted for comparison with another culture. I had done extensive ethnographic and interview research in many communes of the CoG in the United States, plus one each in Canada and France, and the resultant book combined methodologies to understand its history, social structure, and beliefs.[24]

---

[20] Durkheim, E. 1951. *Suicide.* New York, NY: Free Press, 1951. Durkheim, E. 1915. *The Elementary Forms of the Religious Life.* London: Allen and Unwin; Bainbridge, W.S., and R. Stark. 1981. "Suicide, Homicide, and Religion: Durkheim Reassessed." *Annual Review of the Social Sciences of Religion* 5, pp. 33–56; Pickering, W.S.F. 1984. *Durkheim's Sociology of Religion.* London: Routledge and Kegan Paul; Weber, M. 1930. *The Protestant Ethic and the Spirit of Capitalism.* London: G. Allen and Unwin.

[21] Stark, R., and W.S. Bainbridge. 1996. *Religion, Deviance and Social Control.* New York, NY: Routledge.

[22] thearda.com/Archive/Files/Descriptions/BAINCITY.asp

[23] thearda.com/Archive/Files/Descriptions/ENDTIME.asp

[24] Bainbridge, W.S. 2002. *The Endtime Family: Children of God.* Albany, New York, NY: State University of New York Press.

One of the questions asked, "How close do you feel to God most of the time?" Of GSS respondents who answered, 31.8 percent said "extremely close," while 42.1 of CoG gave the same response. The percentages answering "somewhat close" were about the same, 52.5 percent and 51.6 percent, reflecting the fact that the CoG were struggling to get extremely close to God, but many felt they had not yet succeeded. The group's Wikipedia page reports it

> initially spread a message of salvation, apocalypticism, spiritual "revolution and happiness" and distrust of the outside world, which the members called The System. In 1976, it began a method of evangelism called Flirty Fishing, that used sex to "show God's love and mercy" and win converts, resulting in controversy.[25]

Wikipedia even has a page for flirty fishing that calls it

> a form of evangelistic religious prostitution ... The term is derived from Matthew 4:19 from the New Testament, in which Jesus tells two fishermen that he will make them "fishers of men". Cult leader David Berg extrapolated from this that women in his movement should be "flirty fishers" (also called "bait" or "fisherwomen"). The targeted men were called "fish". The cult published several documents with exact instructions. Flirty Fishing was defined as using sex appeal for proselytizing.[26]

Wikipedia is not entirely clear about the fact that the CoG considered sexual intercourse to be a holy act, even perhaps believing that Jesus or God inhabited the souls of any two people of opposite genders, regardless of age, who joined in this way. Thus flirty fishing brought the fisherwomen closer to God, some of them believed. Clearly, this was a different culture from conventional Christianity.

This immediately raises a question: How did the CoG conceptualize their sacred parent? The questionnaire included a dozen items, taken from

---

[25]   en.wikipedia.org/wiki/The_Family_International
[26]   en.wikipedia.org/wiki/Flirty_Fishing

Table 3.5 **Extremely likely an image of God would come to mind**

	GSS males by closeness to God			GSS females by closeness to God			Children of God	
	Extremely	Some what	Not close	Extremely	Some what	Not close	Males	Females
Creator	90.0%	81.5%	56.7%	94.0%	84.9%	46.5%	89.8%	86.6%
Judge	71.6%	46.5%	25.3%	59.8%	43.4%	21.4%	26.4%	17.2%
Redeemer	76.4%	60.9%	27.7%	80.9%	62.4%	24.4%	71.0%	62.4%
Lover	61.1%	43.0%	15.7%	56.8%	40.0%	15.3%	58.4%	62.8%
Master	76.2%	52.3%	29.0%	75.3%	53.4%	23.2%	69.8%	62.6%
Mother	37.5%	20.4%	9.8%	36.2%	23.7%	12.8%	18.6%	15.3%
Father	82.2%	58.6%	25.0%	82.2%	63.1%	33.3%	85.3%	85.2%
Spouse	28.6%	16.6%	6.0%	24.6%	12.2%	8.9%	29.1%	44.7%
Friend	77.4%	56.0%	31.9%	80.2%	66.1%	27.2%	81.3%	86.0%
King	71.5%	48.2%	23.1%	71.4%	50.1%	28.8%	86.5%	86.9%
Liberator	63.7%	39.9%	16.2%	66.2%	40.8%	16.4%	64.2%	60.0%
Healer	84.2%	68.3%	35.1%	87.5%	72.7%	32.3%	76.1%	74.9%
Creator N	432	610	127	622	1,064	314	400	606

the 1983 and 1984 GSS, a set that begins with this question: "When you think about God, how likely are each of these images to come to your mind?" Table 3.5 compares the percentages who responded "extremely likely" in eight subsets of respondents, divided by gender and within the more numerous GSS respondents by how close they feel to God, combining in "not close" three rarer responses: "not very close," "not close at all," and "does not believe" that God exists.

For several of the dozen God descriptors, the CoG respondents gave similar answers to those of the GSS respondents who felt extremely close to God, or between the GSS extremely and somewhat close columns of figures. For example, 90.0 percent of the 432 GSS male respondents who felt extremely close to God said it would be extremely likely that "creator" would come to mind, as did 89.8 percent of 400 CoG males, almost exactly identical fractions. But members of the CoG were very reluctant to conceptualize God as their judge, compared with religious ordinary citizens. This may reflect their history coming out of the counterculture of the 1960s and the unconventional lifestyles members experienced both before and after joining.

Pagan religions of Europe and the Middle East assigned important sacred roles to goddesses and priestesses, while the Judeo-Christian-Islamic tradition conceptualized God as a male—Father rather than Mother— and until recently limited the full role of clergy to men. In today's world, one might expect equality of the supernatural genders again, and at least one Protestant denomination has begun to consider a gender-neutral conception of God.[27] Even around 1997 when the CoG data were collected, and 1983 to 1984 when the GSS data were collected, this discussion had not yet begun. But the CoG members were very unlikely to think of God as their Mother, rather than Father. Among female members of this group, a relatively high percentage could imagine God being their spouse, probably a reflection of the theology behind flirty fishing.

What do the examples of the old U.S. religious censuses, the GSS, and the Association of Religion Data Archives tell us about the future of questionnaire survey research? First, we must face difficult questions about what organizations can legitimately and successfully administer research on cultural topics like religion about which the general public differs. After the 1936 religious census, the U.S. government came to the provisional view that it was unconstitutional for the U.S. government to conduct or support research on religion. The famous First Amendment says,

> Congress shall make no law respecting an establishment of religion, or prohibiting the free exercise thereof; or abridging the freedom of speech, or of the press; or the right of the people peaceably

to assemble, and to petition the Government for a redress of griev-
ances.[28]

Freedom of speech presumably allows social scientists to administer questionnaires or interviews about religion to willing respondents, but concerns were expressed that government support of them could function as
indirect establishment of religion. For that reason, when Charles Glock
and Rodney Stark conducted a major questionnaire study of Anti-Semitism, they could not apply for government support, and had to seek funds
from individual donors instead.[29]

Very few research projects supported by the NSF, other than the GSS
which covers a diversity of topics, concern religion. Entering the word
"God" into the online grant abstract system and reading the results turned
up just 28 research projects, the first dating from 1993. Just 4 of the 28
were studies explicitly of modern religious phenomena, as suggested by
their titles: "Clergy, Parishioners, and Politics: A Survey of ELCA and
Episcopal Church Ministers and Parishioners," "Religious Orthodoxy
and New Media Technologies," "Hearing Religious Language, Making
Political Choices," and "Religion and Financial Market Behavior." The
last two of these were very low budget grants supporting the necessary
costs of a doctoral dissertation research project. Of the 24 other grants,
14 could be described as anthropology or history, and thus do not directly
concern religion in American society today. One does, however, suggest
implications that religion of the past had for the current structure of scientific concepts, reporting the assumption behind the still-significant but
nearly three-century-old Linnaean system for classifying animals: "Lin-
naeus assumed that God created an initial pair of organisms for each species and after God's original creation no new species could arise."[30]

---

[28]   en.wikipedia.org/wiki/First_Amendment_to_the_United_States_Constitu-
tion
[29]   Glock, C.Y., and R. Stark. 1966. *Christian Beliefs and Anti-Semitism*. New
York: Harper and Row.
[30]   www.nsf.gov/awardsearch/showAward?AWD_ID=9310624

The Phenomenological Approach to Ethnography

Scientists tend to place a high value on objectivity, yet research on human culture requires a very personal investment. The posthumous publication of the personal diary of anthropologist Bronislaw Malinowski caused intense controversy, some critics branding him prejudiced and others praising him as a pioneer of "intensive personal fieldwork."[31] Malinowski studied the Trobriand "savages" who lived on islands near New Guinea, while here we shall explore the equally exotic virtual version of New England in *The Secret World* (TSW), a massively multiplayer online role-playing game. As Malinowski well illustrated, cultural anthropology was an intellectual extension of European colonialism in the sense that it viewed indigenous cultures from the perspective of the home culture of the anthropologist, and it was an intellectual corrective to the extent that it took the indigenous culture seriously as a valid perspective in its own right. In the extreme, the home culture of a scientist is not his or her nation, but his or her self. Thus, cultural anthropology is prepared to converge with phenomenology, the most self-centered school of thought. In his 1637 book, *Discourse on the Method*, Descartes presented his influential principle: "I think, therefore I am."[32] That is, one should doubt beliefs unless they are absolutely irrefutable, and one's own existence is a logical precondition for having doubts or any other kind of thoughts.

Three centuries later such Cartesian meditations were the basis of *phenomenology*, which in turn influenced the birth of *ethnomethodology*, perhaps the most individualistic form of sociology, especially as presented by George Psathas, my main teacher when I was an undergraduate at Boston University around 1970. Yet ethnomethodology emphasizes role-playing, so in participant observation research one is able to adopt for research purposes the perspective of a specific other person, for example, a social

---

[31] Wax, M.L. 1972. "Tenting with Malinowski." *American Sociological Review* 37, no. 1, pp. 1–13; Kuklick, H. 2011. "Personal Equations: Reflections on the History of Fieldwork, with Special Reference to Sociocultural Anthropology." *Isis* 102, no. 1, pp. 1–33.

[32] Descartes, R. 1912. *A Discourse on Method*. New York, NY: Dutton.

theorist like Psathas.[33] TSW seemed very appropriate for this kind of phenomenological exploration because it depicts our real world today, but under the assumption that most people are completely ignorant of the horrifying reality that exists just outside their consciousness. Produced by a Norwegian company, it offers rich literary culture in three geographical areas: New England, Egypt, and Transylvania. Especially prominent are American horror writers in the New England tradition, including Nathaniel Hawthorne, Edgar Allan Poe, and Stephen King. Howard Phillips Lovecraft's intellectual influence was the greatest, as symbolized by the fact that a prominent virtual location was an archetype of a New England prep school named Innsmouth Academy, given that Innsmouth was a postapocalyptic town in Lovecraft's mythos that had been attacked by monsters called Deep Ones, an obvious source also for the fictional town in TSW named Kingsmouth.[34]

I decided initially to take the role of my great-grandfather William Folwell Bainbridge, calling the first of three research avatars Folwell. He had been the clergyman for First Baptist Church in Providence, Rhode Island, in the 1870s, had explored Egypt extensively in 1867, and then in 1879 to 1880 did a globe-circling research study of American Protestant Missions and the cultures they sought to convert that resulted in two sociological books.[35] His behavior became erratic, his career and marriage disintegrated, and when he died in 1915 his surgeon son dissected his father's brain seeking exculpatory evidence to soothe this family shame. A powerful connection to the horror variant of phenomenology was symbolized by the fact that he was buried in Swan Point Cemetery, where the body of horror genius Lovecraft would later be interred. In "Surreal Impersonation," an essay about the value of phenomenological fieldwork, I summarized Folwell's findings thus:

---

[33] Bainbridge, W.S. 2016. *Virtual Sociocultural Convergence: Human Sciences of Computer Games.* London: Springer.

[34] en.wikipedia.org/wiki/Innsmouth; en.wikipedia.org/wiki/Deep_One

[35] Bainbridge, W.F. 1882. *Around the World Tour of Christian Missions: A Universal Survey.* New York: C. R. Blackall; Bainbridge, W.F. 1882. *Along the Lines at the Front: A General Survey of Baptist Home and Foreign Missions.* Philadelphia: American Baptist Publication Society.

The past is dead, but lives. To understand the horrors of our existence, we must dig up the past, but full awareness would drive us mad, so we must also bury the past. This theory very much fits the worldview of H. P. Lovecraft, especially his novella, "At the Mountains of Madness," that explores the remains of an ancient civilization in Antarctica, incredibly old, incredibly advanced, and incredibly corrosive of our mundane reality. The work of archaeologists and other scientists is dangerous, Lovecraft asserted, because "some day the piecing together of dissociated knowledge will open up such terrifying vistas of reality, and of our frightful position therein, that we shall either go mad from the revelation or flee from the light into the peace and safety of a new dark age." One of the responsibilities of secret groups like the Illuminati is to prevent ordinary people from learning the truth, and thus being driven insane. Lovecraft once said, "All my tales are based on the fundamental premise that common human laws and interests and emotions have no validity or significance in the vast cosmos at large."[36]

This frankly pessimistic view of life relates to the twin sociological traditions of phenomenology and ethnomethodology in several ways. Lovecraft never was rewarded by publishers or the general public for his profound creativity, dying in abject poverty. Thus his sense that life was meaningless was an empirical finding from his own *personal science*, the active exploration of reality on the basis of one's own private experience. Although not having Lovecraft in mind, Psathas advocated a sociological approach that was a form of personal science:

The distinction between natural science and social science ... is based on the fact that men are not only objects existing in the nat-

---

[36]   Bainbridge, W.S. 2018. "Surreal Impersonation." In *Methods for Studying Video Games and Religion*, eds. V. Sisler, K. Radde-Antweiler, and X. Zeiler, 65–80. New York, NY: Routledge; Lovecraft, H.P. 1928. "The Call of Cthulhu." *Weird Tales* 11, no. 2, pp. 159–178, 287, 159; Carter, P.A. 1977. *The Creation of Tomorrow*, . New York, NY: Columbia University Press.

ural world to be observed by the scientist, but they are creators of a world, a cultural world, of their own. In creating this world, they interpret their own activities. Their overt behavior is only a fragment of their total behavior. Any social scientist who insists that he can understand all of man's behavior by focusing only on that part which is overt and manifested in concrete, directly observable acts is naive, to say the least. The challenge to the social scientist who seeks to understand social reality, then, is to understand the meaning that the actor's act has for him.[37]

In his Boston University classes as well as writings, Psathas referred to publications like *Studies in Ethnomethodology* by Harold Garfinkel, *The Social Construction of Reality* by Peter Berger and Thomas Luckman, and *Cartesian Meditations: An Introduction to Phenomenology* by Edmund Husserl.[38] The classic work that held these radical philosophical statements together was *The Phenomenology of the Social World* by Alfred Schutz.[39] Originally published in German in 1932, this English edition came a third of a century later when the intellectual rebellions of the 1960s were at their peak. Schutz was especially influential in promoting a very radical version of cultural relativism, the concept of *multiple realities*, not only suggesting that each human individual lived in a different universe, but that roles and episodes in each person's life were distinct realities. In a book surveying the sociological literature, I summarized how Schutz considered the large subset of realities that were detached from the intense social interactions of daily life:

---

[37] Psathas, G. 1968. "Ethnomethods and Phenomenology." *Social Research* 35, no. 3, pp. 500–520, 510.

[38] Garfinkel, H. 1967. *Studies in Ethnomethodology*. Englewood Cliffs, New Jersey: Prentice-Hall; Berger, P.L., and T. Luckmann. 1960. *The Social Construction of Reality: A Treatise in the Sociology of Knowledge*. Garden City, New York, NY: Doubleday; Husserl, E. 1960. *Cartesian Meditations: An Introduction to Phenomenology*. The Hague: Martinus Nijhoff.

[39] Schutz, A. 1967. *The Phenomenology of the Social World*. Evanston, Illinois: Northwestern University Press.

A person cannot move smoothly from one of these worlds to another. Rather, a person's consciousness must leap across, and the transition from one reality to another is always a mental shock. Compared with the paramount reality of everyday life, these finite provinces of meaning lack coherent social interaction. The experience of time is different, perhaps utterly so, and we cannot share time coherently with another person. Objects are not stable, and the results of our actions typically vanish. Schutz considers the worlds of *phantasms* (fiction, fantasies, myths, jokes, and the like), dreams, and scientific theory, finding each distinctly different from and yet connected to the world of everyday life.[40]

TSW certainly overflows with phantasms, and with that in mind I created a new avatar named Psathas to explore its reflection of New England again, while I simultaneously surveyed the numerous external phantasms it connected to. There are many ways in which this virtual world is a collection of multiple realities, most notably that it currently exists in two forms, the original 2012 version titled *The Secret World*, and a version with a much simpler interface designed to attract new players, *Secret World Legends* (SWL), that was launched in 2017 and was explored by my Psathas avatar. In addition to Folwell, I already had a secondary avatar in the original TSW, named Dionysius Bainbridge after a probable distant family member who had been the political mentor of his stepson, Guy Fawkes, famous for attempting to destroy the British parliament building in 1605.[41] Wikipedia gives his name as both Dionis Baynbrigge and Denis Bainbridge.[42] In 2015, a musical group called the Gunpowder Plot Conspirators released a memorial piece titled "Farewell Dionis Baynbrigge," illustrated by this band wearing the Guy Fawkes masks associated with hacker-radicals like the online activist Anonymous cabal.[43]

---

[40]   Bainbridge, W.S. 1997. *Sociology*, 73. New York: Barron's.

[41]   De Forest, L.E. 1950. *Ancestry of William Seaman Bainbridge*, 8. Oxford: Scrivener Press.

[42]   en.wikipedia.org/wiki/Guy_Fawkes

[43]   thegunpowderplotconspirators.bandcamp.com/track/farewell-dionis-baynbrigge

Table 3.6 Three parallel explorations of a virtual reality

Description	Folwell	Dionysius	Psathas
Location exploration sites:			
Solomon Island (New England)	65	25	58
Valley of the Sun God (Egypt)	66	0	0
Transylvania (Romania)	97	0	0
Legend fragments learned (lore):			
Solomon Island (New England)	55	9	51
Valley of the Sun God (Egypt)	22	0	0
Transylvania (Romania)	1	0	0
Missions completed:			
Kingsmouth Town (Solomon Island)	55	20	41
The Savage Coast (Solomon Island)	46	0	39
The Blue Mountain (Solomon Island)	27	0	25
The Scorched Desert (Valley of the Sun God)	33	0	0
City of the Sun God (Valley of the Sun God)	16	0	0
Transylvania	0	0	0
Humanoid monsters killed in New England:			
Zombies: animated corpses lacking self-awareness	2,657	4,356	2,063
Familiars: former companions of students of magic	555	724	455
Draug: the cause of a hundred ghost ship tales	282	328	239
Rakshasa: demons in the Hindu–Buddhist tradition	116	0	29
Spectres: terrible mass, terrifying physicality	109	89	90
Wendigo: cannibal vestiges of humans	104	4	56
Filthy Humans: driven mad by an epidemic disease	70	1	48
Golems: monsters created from inanimate matter	39	2	43
Deep Ones: from the cold depths of the Atlantic	33	0	41
Shades: evil ghosts who escaped the underworld	33	0	26
Scarecrows: manifestations of fear and hatred	30	0	30
Revanants: craving misery, pestilence, and death	14	1	8

In order to compare the very different interface systems and the contrasting sets of variables that define the avatar's characteristics, I revived Dionysius in New England, alternating him with Psathas, as they attempted to explore their different realities in the same geography. Since I was already familiar with the original interface, I added the experiment of seeing how difficult it was for Dionysius to progress without taking on any more missions for nonplayer characters (NPCs), even as Psathas did as many missions as he could to document his interactions with friendly NPCs. Table 3.6 reports that Folwell visited all 228 areas available in the three regions of this virtual world, while Dionysius and Psathas were limited to locations in New England, Dionysius visiting far fewer because he had no motivation to wander in search of missions to perform. Fragments of legends could be learned by finding a bright node somewhere in the geography and touching it. Dionysius killed 5,505 monsters in New England, rather more than the 4,042 by Folwell or 3,128 by Psathas, because that was the only way he could gain experience or equipment because he earned no further mission or lore rewards.

Psathas paid close attention to the process of receiving missions and being rewarded when he completed them. Location exploration simply meant going to a particular small area within a region, and Folwell found all of them in all three lands. Thus, no social interaction was required. Also distributed across the landscape were nodes where pieces of text could be collected, which assembled into lore-based legends. Commenting on a blogsite article, Hikari Kenzaki wrote: "Secret World Legends has some wonderfully confusing lore. I say wonderfully because it's intended to confuse you. Your handlers and even the Buzzing will outright lie to you through the course of the game."[44] *Handlers* are the high-status NPCs that give orders to the player's avatar, usually lore-related, within one of three mutually tolerant factions: the Illuminati in New York City, the Templars in London, and the Dragons in Seoul, Korea. The legend fragments are like scraps of paper torn from a book, thus impersonal whoever the author may have been. Handlers may be interacted with in person or

---

[44]   massivelyop.com/2019/03/30/the-daily-grind-which-mmos-lore-confuses-you

at a distance, but are personified. The Buzzing are multizone, cross-faction, and mysterious:

> We are the Education Protocol. We climb the twisted ladder of your cells; we haunt your digital text; we hide in your hat. We are the jagged teeth that trip the tumblers of your mind. You will not know our triggers. For all the world's a cypher. And everything is true.[45]

Many missions are given by local NPCs, more or less separately from the faction-centered handlers. Innsmouth Academy is clearly connected to the Illuminati, yet its staff have their own needs, chiefly protection against familiars, a subclass of zombies who were former companions of students of magic. Some NPCs are more economic in function, buying and selling equipment or potions that confer special powers. A player's avatar may craft equipment, usually from raw materials obtained by processing other pieces of equipment looted from defeated enemies. Other NPCs may be called *extras*, by analogy with the crowds in movies who lack names or important roles, sometimes relevant to missions, but often merely standing in the background. Another category is *departed characters*, whether they died or simply ran away, who left artifacts such as cell phones bearing messages that would give the avatar a mission.

Missions usually require killing enemies, but it is also easy to gain experience points and resources by killing enemies without any complex story. Some of them function individually, while others are in teams of two, three, or four, who must be battled simultaneously. Both inside and outside missions there are *boss characters*, individual enemies who are dangerous and difficult to kill. Some are animals or mysterious lights in the air, but Table 3.4 lists the total of 12,675 humanoid monsters I killed in New England, not to tally all the mummies Folwell killed in Egypt. Now that I am no longer playing Folwell, Dionysius, and Psathas, perhaps they have joined the ranks of the familiars, and plague today's students at Innsmouth Academy. I am left contemplating the culture of my native New

---

45   thesecretworldguide.weebly.com/buzzing.html

England, in the so-called real world, counting the bosses and lights in the air I personally encountered. More generally, the New England horror literature tradition is really a major part of the region's dominant culture, and the Choate School I attended was not very different from Innsmouth Academy.

Observing Cultural Structure Statistically Through Interlocks

Research on the social structure of industries has often traced interlocking directorates, the ties between corporations represented by people who hold leadership positions in two or more.[46] In my earlier book in this series, *Virtual Local Manufacturing Communities*, I analyzed the membership connections between guilds in *A Tale in the Desert*, an online social simulation of the construction of Ancient Egypt.[47] Unlike most online games, *Tale* does not allow violence, does not require membership in hostile factions, and therefore permits each person to belong to many groups. The research focus was on how group membership was a function of two factors, the functions of the groups and their geographic distribution across a huge simulated Egypt. This methodology can be applied as well to the study of online communities that are focused on genres of culture, and here we will illustrate this opportunity through a cluster of Facebook groups oriented toward the 1967 to 1968 British television series *The Prisoner* that dramatizes many of the dangers that humanists believe information technology presents to humanity.

---

[46]   Allen, M.P. 1974. "The Structure of Interorganizational Elite Cooptation: Interlocking Corporate Directorates." *American Sociological Review* 39, no. 3, pp. 393–406; Zajac, E.J. 1988. "Interlocking Directorates as an Interorganizational Strategy: A Test of Critical Assumptions." *The Academy of Management Journal* 31, no. 2, pp. 428–438; Kono, C., D. Palmer, R. Friedland, and M. Zafonte. 1998. "Lost in Space: The Geography of Corporate Interlocking Directorates." *American Journal of Sociology* 103, no. 4, pp. 863–911; Granovetter, M. 2017. *Society and Economy.* Cambridge, Massachusetts: Harvard University Press.

[47]   Bainbridge, W.S. 2019. *Virtual Local Manufacturing Communities: Online Simulations of Future Workshop Systems.* Business Expert Press.

Patrick McGoohan, co-creator of the series, played the role of a person named only Number 6, who is held captive in a beautiful but mysterious seaside location named The Village, as a sequence of dictators named Number 2 seek to control his mind. The main Wikipedia page for *The Prisoner* had 1,123,086 views, July 1, 2015, through March 1, 2019; the page listing the 17 episodes had 199,940, and a page about the mysterious village where Number 6 is imprisoned had 100,493.[48] A common salutation spoken by many characters, "Be seeing you," is reminiscent of "Big Brother is watching you" from George Orwell's novel *Nineteen Eighty-Four*.[49] Each episode begins with the following opening sequence:

Number Six: Where am I?

Number Two (not identified as yet): In the village.

Six: What do you want?

Two: Information.

Six: Whose side are you on?

Two: That would be telling. We want information ...information ... information!!!

Six: You won't get it!

Two: By hook or by crook, we will.

Six: Who are you?

Two: The new Number Two.

Six: Who is Number One?

Two: You are Number Six.

Six (running on the Village's beach): I am not a number; I am a free man!!!

Two: [Laughter][50]

---

[48] en.wikipedia.org/wiki/The_Prisoner; en.wikipedia.org/wiki/List_of_The_Prisoner_episodes; en.wikipedia.org/wiki/The_Village_(The_Prisoner)

[49] en.wikipedia.org/wiki/Big_Brother_(Nineteen_Eighty-Four)

[50] en.wikipedia.org/wiki/Opening_and_closing_sequences_of_The_Prisoner

The largest Facebook group devoted to *The Prisoner*, as of April 18, 2019, was simply named The Prisoner, with 6,648 identifiable members, 1,864 of whom had been members for "about 10 years" or longer. Officially, Facebook was launched on February 4, 2004, in the United States and expanded to other nations in the following year.[51] Thus it is remarkable that The Prisoner group was created on December 3, 2004, so early in the history of this social medium. The FB profile of the founder, David Bowers, suggests he had just graduated from high school and was a freshman at Pennsylvania State University, thus indicating how The Prisoner group harmonized initially with the original focus of Facebook on college students. He continues to be listed as one of three admins of the group, the other two apparently more active at the present time. Anthony Rooney joined the group on September 16, 2007, and by 2013 had taken the main responsibility for adding new members. The third admin, Shane Poole, joined much later, on October 5, 2014, but has been very active, notably serving as Podcast Host at In the Village.[52] Its goal is to teach newcomers about the subculture, being an "introcast about the classic tv show The Prisoner that ran from 1967-1968. Join our newbies as they discover the mystery of the village for the very first time."[53] The Prisoner's "about" page asks "What's it all about?" then offers this introduction:

> When a man resigns from a highly classified job, he is abducted to a mysterious location known only as The Village, where his captors try to find out the reasons for his resignation. Has he been imprisoned by his own side, trying to protect their secrets, or is it the other side trying to extract them? The Prisoner, now unwillingly designated "Number Six," must fight to retain his own identity in a society geared to total sublimation of the individual, while making unceasing efforts to escape.[54]

---

[51] en.wikipedia.org/wiki/Facebook

[52] www.facebook.com/prisonerintrocast

[53] theprisonerintrocast.podbean.com

[54] www.facebook.com/groups/2200730713/about

Currently it is possible to purchase *The Complete Prisoner Megaset* of DVDs from Amazon.com for $250, and the site indicates their original publication date was September 25, 2001. If one has a Prime membership with Amazon, one can watch online for free. However, two sources uploaded the 17-episode series for free viewing at YouTube. As of March 1, 2019, each episode had its own Wikipedia page, with a total of 475,971 pageviews, and on the two YouTube channels they had received 219,779 and 135,704 views, respectively. After joining nine Facebook groups devoted to *The Prisoner*, I posted this question: "What do you think of the fact that all episodes are freely available on YouTube now, apparently uploaded by people ... who believe the copyright ran out after 50 years?" A veteran member replied, "The copyright hasn't run out, it will run out 75 years after the death of the last director (so around 2084). The series is copyright ITV Global Entertainment." Indeed, when I checked back three months later, both sets of videos had been removed from YouTube. It is ironic that one can borrow books and physical videos for free from lending libraries, but online sharing may violate copyright, or as the current rhetoric calls them, *intellectual property rights*. Arguably, prior to industrialization all elements of culture were shared, and intellectual property rights did not exist. Patents and copyrights were necessary to promote creativity and hard work during the era of mass production. Now that we have entered postindustrial society, some writers suggest it is time to again permit unlimited sharing.[55]

Dutiful residents of The Village often criticized Number 6 for being *unmutual*, meaning that he refused to freely share everything with everyone. If we want information, one good place to get it is The Unmutual, *The Prisoner* news website.[56] As of May 20, 2019, its history page lists 813 major updates since it launched April 10, 2004, "as replacement for the old 'tripod' Unmutual site." It links to other websites, fan fiction, and a vast diversity of essays about *The Prisoner*. A page listing local clubs begins:

---

[55] Bainbridge, W.S. 2003. "Privacy and Property on the Net: Research Questions." *Science* 302, pp. 1686–1687.

[56] theunmutual.co.uk/index.htm

For many years, various "Prisoner Local Groups" have been active across the UK. These are small informal meetings (usually in pubs) where fans can attend to socialize with other Prisoner enthusiasts who share their interests. None of the groups listed here require membership to any fan club or society, and are not controlled by any such committee. If you have an easy going outlook and don't want the narrow intensity of fans who take The Prisoner far too seriously then these are the meetings for you.[57]

Here our emphasis is on the nine Facebook groups, virtual clubs that take *The Prisoner* at least somewhat seriously, listed here in descending order of size and giving their years of creation:

1. The Prisoner (2004) "dedicated to the classic Sixties TV series created by and starring PATRICK McGOOHAN."
2. The Prisoner & Portmeirion (2015) "A group for fans of The Prisoner and the village of Portmeirion, setting of the cult '60s TV series."
3. The Prisoner & Patrick McGoohan Memorabilia Group (2016) "This group is for Memorabilia related to the TV series The Prisoner and the actor Patrick McGoohan who was The Prisoner and did many films and TV series."
4. Everything McGoohan (2016) "This group is for everything Patrick McGoohan has been involved with or about people he has worked with. Also for discussion about Portmeirion and anything that was made there!"
5. The Prisoner (1967–68) TV Series, Including Danger Man (2014) "A Group to discuss aspects of the Classic 60's Television Series the Prisoner, Starring Patrick McGoohan as Number 6 with various guest actors as Number 2. Now including all series of Danger Man from the earliest half hour Episodes up to the two colour episodes Koroshi and Shinda Shima."
6. Patrick McGoohan (2008) "For fans of Danger Man star and Prisoner creator, Patrick McGoohan."

---

[57] theunmutual.co.uk/localgroups.htm

7. Patrick McGoohan is ... Danger Man !! (2015) "Danger Man, featuring the talents of the great Patrick McGoohan as John Drake, was a British TV series produced (& transmitted) between 1959 & 1968. The series was also a success in the USA, being shown there under the name 'Secret Agent'."

8. Portmeirion & The Prisoner Memories (2017) "Its our family album to share your snaps. This space is for lovers of Portmeirion and the cult 60's TV series 'The Prisoner.' Portmeirion is located in North Wales and this was the location used for filming 'The Prisoner.'"

9. When is PMG on your TV? (2018) "When is PMG (Patrick McGoohan) on your TV is to let every PMG fan know when he is on TV and also to let us know when you are watching him on your device!"

Portmeirion is the name of the more-or-less real Village where the series was filmed, and *Danger Man* is the name of the earlier spy-oriented adventure series Patrick McGoohan had starred in, called *Secret Agent* in the United States, and that provided some background. To get a sense of

Table 3.7 Nine Facebook groups that dwell in the village

	Group 1	Group 2	Group 3	Group 4	Group 5	Group 6	Group 7	Group 8	Group 9
Group 1	6577	24.9%	24.7%	25.1%	24.2%	25.1%	19.9%	28.8%	21.9%
Group 2	904	2508	28.9%	27.8%	23.7%	19.3%	21.0%	38.0%	28.7%
Group 3	490	460	1166	33.3%	21.8%	22.2%	20.6%	34.5%	31.7%
Group 4	444	405	363	1024	28.7%	28.1%	30.7%	30.9%	35.3%
Group 5	341	285	205	256	790	20.1%	26.8%	22.5%	23.1%
Group 6	351	230	208	249	158	781	27.1%	18.2%	21.8%
Group 7	171	163	136	195	156	157	460	15.5%	25.4%
Group 8	163	201	163	142	97	78	56	296	30.7%
Group 9	35	45	48	53	34	32	35	39	81

how these groups connected into a subculture, I copied the names of all their members, with data about which groups each person belonged to. A total of 9,796 people are represented in this dataset, and 7,746 belong to only 1 of the 9 groups. Another 1,160 belong to 2 groups, and 433 belong to 3. The remainder are rather deeply embedded in this subculture: 202 to 4 groups, 123 to 5 groups, 68 to 6 groups, 35 to 7 groups, 19 to 8 groups, and 10 people belong to all 9 groups. Table 3.7 summarizes this structure.

The diagonal from upper left to lower right gives the membership of each group, slightly lower than the totals one sees at the main Facebook page for each, 6,577 rather than 6,648 in the case of the biggest Group 1, removing a few with multiple identities and others who apparently wished greater privacy. The numbers below and to the left of that diagonal are the members of one group that also belonged to the other, 904 member *interlocks* in the case of the first two groups. The numbers above and to the right express the interlocks as the average percentage of the two groups: 904 is 13.745 percent of 6,577 and 36.045 percent of 2,508; the average of those two percentages, rounded off, is 24.9 percent.

The most important finding is that the interlock percentages are substantial, ranging from 15.5 percent to 38.0 percent, keeping in mind that randomly selected Facebook groups of this size range would tend to have 0.0 percent interlocks. The 38.0 percent interlock is between the two groups that have Portmeirion in their names, indicating that people with a strong interest in the real Village might join both. The second highest interlock is between two groups focused on Patrick McGoohan, and that also have the same administrators. So, the differences in the interlock percentages are meaningful. But the main observation is that all the interlocks are strong enough to indicate that this is a coherent subculture.

Conclusion

Each example of quantitative data summarized in this chapter has some value for mapping a subculture, yet the unit of analysis varied. The GSS was not a random sample of individuals, but interviewed clusters of respondents in a representative set of geographic locations; the CoG respondents were opinion leaders within a radical religious movement;

Bandcamp and ReverbNation posters were ambitious musicians, and the meaning of membership in Facebook groups varies from person to person and group to group. These observations refute the hope of decades past that absolutely objective science can be done via surveys, yet the data remain valuable through convergence of humanities and the social information sciences. Instead of relying upon one or two professional critics to describe an artwork or genre to us, we can use methods like surveys to gain much richer multidimensional descriptions. Each research method has its own limitations, yet they offer researchers a diversity of choices when planning a study, and may be combined in many ways. Adding the phenomenological approach to the mix, we can realize that it can be valid and valuable to chart how a subculture relates to ourselves, placing the researchers on the map beside the cultists and musicians, even counting the interlocks between groups of sociologists, artists, and computer programmers.

CHAPTER 4

Computer Simulations and Creative Theory

Decades ago, several computationally sophisticated social theorists believed that computer simulations, many of which employed artificial intelligence principles, could be used to test and improve the rigor of theories in the social sciences. Examples include books like *World Dynamics* (1971) by Jay Forrester, *Micromotives and Macrobehavior* (1978) by Thomas Schelling, and *The Evolution of Cooperation* (1984) by Robert Axelrod.[1] Although a European journal exists in this area, *The Journal of Artificial Societies and Social Simulation*, and other journals sometimes publish social simulation studies, this methodology has not become a common tool for theorizing in sociology, political science, and anthropology, despite some popularity in economics. Emergence of a coherent yet creative cultural science will require tools for theorizing as well as for analyzing data. This chapter will consider the options in two ways: (1) consideration of how suitable many classic sociological theories are for computer simulation and (2) exploration of how an intellectually sophisticated commercial computer game can represent multiple ideologies.

Simulation of Religious Culture

The term *artificial intelligence* has many meanings. Currently, much of the research excitement concerns forms of *machine learning*, including *deep neural networks* in which a complex pattern of real-number weights

---

[1] Forrester, J.W. 1971. *World Dynamics*. Cambridge, Massachusetts: Wright-Allen Press; Schelling, T.C. 1978. *Micromotives and Macrobehavior*. New York, NY: Norton; Axelrod, R. 1984. *The Evolution of Cooperation*. New York, NY: Basic Books.

on the connections between nodes in the memory structure adjusts the network's output on the basis of the input of complex data. But very different definitions include *rule-based reasoning*, in which a structure of predefined formal relationships allows abstract analysis of different situations. I have found both approaches to be of value in the development of sociological theories and in testing their logical coherence and predictive rigor, in addition of course to empirical tests of the extent to which a theory describes the real world. Here we summarize a compatible set of social theories that were originally framed as sequential lists of formal rules, thus very suitable for rule-based simulations. However, we begin by noting that different AI methods can be combined, just as an individual's mental processes are a fundamental component of social influence.

Social theory development by means of neural nets does not necessarily mean getting accurate predictions, because the goal is to model human thinking which often incorporates errors or imaginative additions to reality, as in the case of literature and drama. In a 1995 issue of *The Journal of Mathematical Sociology*, I presented results from a program I jokingly called MIND: Minimum Intelligent Neural Device, showing how an intentionally limited neural net could model human ethnic prejudice:

> A simple but effective neural network algorithm illustrates common principles of this new class of computational tools. Designed for use in a range of simulation studies, this minimum intelligent neural device is capable of learning which of a complex set of stimuli to avoid, and large numbers of these devices can be assembled in programs to explore the development of prejudice and of various interaction strategies. Neural nets are error-reduction algorithms with the potential to perform a wide range of useful tasks, including modeling theories of the social consequences of human error.[2]

This somewhat defective MIND was based on Gordon Allport's theory of cognitive effort that avoiding prejudice requires mental work. In this simulation, misbehavior by a few people we interact with need not

---

[2]   Bainbridge, W.S. 1995. "Minimum Intelligent Neural Device: A Tool for Social Simulation." *The Journal of Mathematical Sociology* 20, pp. 179–192.

force us to avoid all members of their group, but to make more careful distinctions among them.[3] The neural net could solve the problems presented to it, but it was specifically designed to do so only with difficulty.

Beginning with journal articles published in 1979 and 1980, Rodney Stark and I had been developing a general sociocognitive theory of religion that concerned both how individual human minds conceptualized the supernatural and how people interacted to create religious movements and organizations. In the 1960s, Stark had worked with senior sociologist of religion, Charles Glock, doing research primarily using questionnaire data. One of their books focused on a specific kind of cultural prejudice, *Christian Beliefs and Anti-Semitism.*[4] In a 1965 article, Stark collaborated with John Lofland to offer a theory of the emergence of religious subcultures, integrating concepts from a well-established theoretical tradition.[5] Their theoretical model could be applied to a wide range of subcultures, but was presented as a series of steps an individual must go through in order to convert from conventional religion to a radical cult or sect. Each step could be modeled as a procedure in a computer program, although the authors presented the model as a structure for human cognition. The recruit to a radical religious group must:

1. Experience enduring, acutely felt tensions,
2. Within a religious problem-solving perspective,
3. Which leads him to define himself as a religious seeker;
4. Encountering the group at a turning point in his life
5. Wherein an affective bond is formed (or pre-exists) with one or more converts;
6. Where extra-cult attachments are absent or neutralized;
7. And where, if he is to become a deployable agent, he is exposed to intensive interaction.

---

[3] Allport, G. 1954. *The Nature of Prejudice.* Boston: Beacon Press.

[4] Glock, C.Y., and R. Stark. 1966. *Christian Beliefs and Anti-Semitism.* New York, NY: Harper and Row.

[5] Lofland, J., and R. Stark. 1965. "Becoming a World-Saver: A Theory of Conversion to a Deviant Perspective." *American Sociological Review* 30, pp. 862–875; Lofland, J. 1966. *Doomsday Cult.* Englewood Cliffs, New Jersey: Prentice-Hall.

The first step in the Lofland–Stark theory came from the *strain theory* of Robert Merton and Neil Smelser that people will deviate from standard norms and join or create new cultural movements only when they are dissatisfied with their current life situation.[6] A neural net can represent "acutely felt tensions," by having a suboptimal model of external contingencies, such that the variable measuring success is declining or negative. Step 2 in the theory observes that people may function within a broader cultural context, for example, conceptualizing social problems in religious, political, or psychiatric terms. An especially sophisticated program could represent these alternatives in a neural net, allowing a simulated individual to abandon one problem-solving perspective and learn another, through social interaction, although that was not a feature of the Lofland–Stark model. Steps 5 through 7 of the model are a simplification of one version of *differential association theory*, developed by Edwin Sutherland. It could be applied to many kinds of human behavior, perhaps all kinds that could be described as culture, but was aimed at criminology. As summarized by Sutherland in 1947, it described a series of symbolic interaction steps that would result in commission of crimes:[7]

1. Criminal behavior is learned from other individuals.
2. Criminal behavior is learned in interaction with other persons in a process of communication.
3. The principal part of the learning of criminal behavior occurs within intimate personal groups.
4. When criminal behavior is learned, the learning includes (a) techniques of committing the crime, which are sometimes very complicated, sometimes simple; (b) the specific direction of motives, drives, rationalizations, and attitudes.
5. The specific direction of motives and drives is learned from definitions of the legal codes as favorable or unfavorable.

---

[6]   Merton, R.K. 1968. *Social Theory and Social Structure*. New York, NY: Free Press: Smelser, N.J. 1962. *Theory of Collective Behavior*. New York, NY: Free Press.
[7]   Sutherland, E.H. 1947. *Principles of Criminology*. Philadelphia: Lippincott.

6. A person becomes delinquent because of an excess of definitions favorable to violation of law over definitions unfavorable to violation of the law.

7. Differential associations may vary in frequency, duration, priority, and intensity.

8. The process of learning criminal behavior by association with criminal and anticriminal patterns involves all of the mechanisms that are involved in any other learning.

9. While criminal behavior is an expression of general needs and values, it is not explained by those needs and values, since noncriminal behavior is an expression of the same needs and values.

This is a marvelously rich theoretical statement, but it has often been interpreted too narrowly to state that people become criminals simply because their friends are already criminals. It is too easy to read *associations* as friendships or social relations more broadly. However, as clearly explained in a later edition of Sutherland's criminology textbook, associations can mean mental associations between concepts.[8] Successful criminals must have skills required to commit their particular crimes, the *techniques* mentioned in step 4 of the theory, and those include cognitive abilities the individual can learn from other people. Skills are significant features of most subcultures, such as criminal gangs, classical music orchestras, and the Chicago School of Sociology to which Sutherland belonged. The learning also involves "the specific direction of motives, drives, rationalizations, and attitudes," each of which can be one of the "definitions" that the subcultures employ to understand and exploit the world.

Thus, while focused on social groups, this theory is highly cognitive in nature and does not actually require the individual to learn through face-to-face interaction. It may be that criminal behavior is so difficult and so dangerous that only strong social influence, perhaps in the context of wider social disorganization, can complete the process of learning. But for many other kinds of subculture, the mode of communication could be

---

[8]   Sutherland, E.H., and D.R. Cressey. 1974. *Criminology*. Philadelphia: Lippincott.

reading novels, watching movies, and scanning online social media. We could restate step 6 in terms of any subculture, such as: A person becomes a sci-fi fan because of an excess of definitions favorable to science fiction over definitions unfavorable to science fiction. How would this happen? "Differential associations may vary in frequency, duration, priority, and intensity." Watching *Star Wars* in impressionable childhood (priority meaning earlier in life) and happening to see all the other unusually exciting (intensity) sci-fi films of that period (frequency and duration) could explain becoming an avid adult reader of science fiction novels.

When Stark and I collaborated, I naturally added my own theoretical background to his. At that point, I had written my first two books. My doctoral dissertation was a primarily historical study of the social movement that caused governments to invest in developing space rockets, and I still tend to see science and technology as cultures that become social movements in their more dynamic stages.[9] My second book was more like cultural anthropology, an ethnographic field study of a radical religious movement that had formed from a pre-existing network of college students and artists. Having the Sutherland and Lofland–Stark models in mind, I described the formation of the group as a social implosion: "In a *social implosion*, part of an extended social network collapses as social ties within it strengthen and, reciprocally, those to persons outside it weaken. It is a step by step process."[10]

Also in mind was the theory of my main teacher in graduate school, George Homans. He was a personal friend of B.F. Skinner, and accepted the fundamental Behaviorist principles in Skinner's 1938 book *The Behavior of Organisms*.[11] He was also inspired by the 1939 book *Frustration and Aggression*, by John Dollard, Neal Miller, and their colleagues, that considered the cognitive consequences of failure to achieve one's desires, but in a manner more compatible with Behaviorism than the

[9]   Bainbridge, W.S. 1976. *The Spaceflight Revolution*. New York, NY: Wiley Interscience.

[10]   Bainbridge, W.S. 1978. *Satan's Power: A Deviant Psychotherapy Cult*, 51–52. Berkeley: University of California Press.

[11]   Skinner, B.F. 1938. *The Behavior of Organisms*. New York, NY: Appleton-Century Company.

Merton-Smelser framework.[12] Homans developed his own form of Socio-logical Behaviorism, beginning with his 1950 book, *The Human Group*, where he postulated that people who interact rewardingly with each other repeatedly will come both to value each other and to become more similar to each other.[13] Note the emphasis on *rewards* rather than the *associations* in Sutherland's theory. In its fully developed form, communicated in the 1974 edition of his book *Social Behavior: Its Elementary Forms*, Homans began with a small set of axioms he called *propositions*:[14]

1. For all actions taken by persons, the more often a particular action of a person is rewarded, the more likely the person is to perform that action.

2. If in the past the occurrence of a particular stimulus, or set of stimuli has been the occasion on which a person's action has been rewarded, then the more similar the present stimuli are to the past ones, the more likely the person is to perform the action, or some similar action, now.

3. The more valuable to a person is the result of his action, the more likely he is to perform the action.

4. The more often in the recent past a person has received a particular reward, the less valuable any further unit of that reward becomes for him.

5A. When a person's action does not receive the reward he expected, or receives punishment he did not expect, he will be angry; he becomes more likely to perform aggressive behavior, and the results of such behavior become more valuable to him.

5B. When a person's action receives reward he expected, especially a greater reward than he expected, or does not receive punishment he expected, he will be pleased; he becomes more likely to perform

[12]   Dollard, J., N.E. Miller, L.W. Doob, O.H. Mowrer, and R.R. Sears. 1939. *Frustration and Aggression*. New Haven: Yale University Press.

[13]   Homans, G.C. 1950. *The Human Group*. New York, NY: Harcourt, Brace and World.

[14]   Homans, G.C. 1974. *Social Behavior: Its Elementary Forms*. New York, NY: Harcourt, Brace, Jovanovich.

approving behavior, and the results of such behavior become more valuable to him.

The first proposition merely states the starting point for Skinnerian Behaviorist theory. The second proposition twice uses the word *similar*, which refers to a cognitive judgment by a human mind, and provides a starting point for a theory of art, although I do not recall Homans developing this line of analysis. A crude example is that people learn to seek fruit to eat, because it is tasty and satisfies hunger, so they may come to like pictures of fruit as well, despite their lack of nutritional value. A more complex example may explain the popularity of computer games. In real life, people learn they must compete against each other in order to gain a variety of material rewards and also the instrumental reward of social status that helps them gain rewards of many kinds. The games are somewhat realistic, including gaining status with simulated human beings and a bank account of simulated money. Thus popular games tend to be somewhat similar to reality.

The fourth proposition relates to the arts in a different way. When a person frequently succeeds in gaining a particular reward, it becomes less valuable, at least in the short term until the person runs out of it. That liberates the person's mind to seek some other reward. While rich people may consume more costly food than poor people, they are also able to afford rewards of lower practical value, such as artworks. This option can illustrate itself through a cute pun rather than an ugly proposition: truffles versus trifles. An elite cooking school has even named itself Truffles and Trifles.[15] However, all of the arts deserve to be taken seriously, and practically all of them have traditionally been connected to religion, from literature like the bible, to Gregorian chant music, to Salvador Dali's surreal painting of the crucifixion. Or should that word be *crucifiction*?

Even without invoking the term *sacred*, religion is among the very most significant aspects of human culture. Debates about the truth of particular religious beliefs are both socially antagonistic and intellectually profound. For example, Harvard philosopher and psychologist William James argued for a pragmatic definition of truth: "The true is the name of

---

15   trufflesandtrifles.com

whatever proves itself to be good in the way of belief, and good, too, for definite, assignable reasons."[16] "'The true' to put it very briefly, is only the expedient in the way of our thinking, just as 'the right' is only the expedient in our way of behaving."[17] If religious beliefs serve valuable functions for human beings, then for that reason they are true. When Stark and I began collaborating in the development of a formal theory of religion, we gave each other some room to hold different views on the truth of religious beliefs, but the resultant theory is consistent with the view that religion is an artform, comprised of metaphors and imagination, rather than being a system either of firm beliefs or statements of fact. We began with a slightly different set of axioms than those proposed by Homans[18]:

1. Human perception and action take place through time, from the past into the future.
2. Humans seek what they perceive to be rewards and avoid what they believe to be costs.
3. Rewards vary in kind, value, and generality.
4. Human action is directed by a complex but finite information-processing system that functions to identity problems and identify solutions to them.
5. Some desired rewards are limited in supply, including some that simply do not exist.
6. Most rewards sought by humans are destroyed when they are used.
7. Individual and social attributes which determine power are unequally distributed among persons and groups in any society.

In the form presented in our 1987 book, *A Theory of Religion*, these seven axioms provided the basis for 344 hypotheses we suggested (but did not fully demonstrate) could be derived as theorems from these axioms,

---

[16] James, W. 1907. *Pragmatism*, 76. New York, NY: Longmans, Green.

[17] James, W. 1907. *Pragmatism*, 222. New York, NY: Longmans, Green.

[18] Stark, R., and W.S. Bainbridge. 1978. *A Theory of Religion*, 325. New York, NY: Toronto/Lang. Stark, R., and W.S. Bainbridge. 1980. "Towards a Theory of Religion: Religious Commitment." *Journal for the Scientific Study of Religion* 19, pp. 114–128.

within a framework of 104 definitions of concepts. It is a highly cognitive theory, and the last three axioms place the human mind in a world where rewards are limited, thus presenting people with dynamic challenges in their attempt to gain rewards. Because rewards vary in "vary in kind, value, and generality," so do human plans to gain this diversity of rewards. The original statement of this theory used the term *explanations* to refer to such plans, although in my computer simulation research the term *algorithms* seemed appropriate as well. Here is the subset of definitions, originally presented in a chain of theorems, which will not be quoted here, that led to the emergence of religion in human culture:

Def.10: *Explanations* are statements about how and why rewards may be obtained and costs are incurred.

Def.18: *Compensators* are postulations of reward according to explanations that are not readily susceptible to unambiguous evaluation.

Def.19: Compensators which substitute for single, specific rewards are called *specific compensators*.

Def.20: Compensators which substitute for a cluster of many rewards and for rewards of great scope and value are called *general compensators*.

Def.21: *Supernatural* refers to forces beyond or outside nature which can suspend, alter, or ignore physical forces.

Def.22: *Religion* refers to systems of general compensators based on supernatural assumptions.

Def.23: *Religious organizations* are social enterprises whose primary purpose is to create, maintain, and exchange supernaturally based general compensators.

Def.52: *Magic* refers to specific compensators that promise to provide desired rewards without regard for evidence concerning the designated means.

Def.57: A *sect movement* is a deviant religious organization with traditional beliefs and practices.

Def.58: A *cult movement* is a deviant religious organization with novel beliefs and practices.

Def.67: *Cults* are social enterprises primarily engaged in the generation and exchange of novel compensators.

In the context of cultural science, "Cult is culture writ small." The theory is not limited to primitive magic or traditional religion, but extends to all forms of artistic culture. Watching Luke Skywalker wield his light sabre in a *Star Wars* movie provides vicarious rewards, perhaps a feeling of self-esteem if we identify with him, but does not require belief that his powers are real. In an earlier book about how religion is depicted in online virtual world, I observed:

> Religion has always been deeply implicated in the creative arts, but the relationships among them are changing. Perhaps we shall come to see religion merely as an especially solemn artform. Suspension of disbelief is the essence of art, according to Samuel Taylor Coleridge, and electronic games are a new and powerful artform that often depicts religion. Yet we may wonder whether suspension of disbelief is really very different from belief itself.[19]

In the most complex of my religion simulations, I assembled several similar procedures that learned how to achieve different rewards, with a simple but higher-level procedure that would decide which reward the simulated person wanted at the moment. When rewards were unavailable, the model could become very imprecise, no longer able to distinguish fact (obtaining a reward) from fiction (responding as if a reward had been received).

---

[19] Bainbridge, W.S. 2013. *eGods: Faith Versus Fantasy in Computer Gaming*, 3–4. New York, NY: Oxford University Press: cf: Wuthnow, R. 2009. "The Contemporary Convergence of Art and Religion." In *The Oxford Handbook of the Sociology of Religion*, eds P.B. Clarke. Oxford, 360–374. England: Oxford University Press: Coleridge, S.T. 1817. *Biographia Literaria*. New York, NY: Kirk and Merein.

Simulation of Sociocultural Influences

In several earlier studies of cultural dynamics, using computer simulation methods, I showed how the combination of Sutherland's differential
association theory and an alternative theory offered by Fritz Heider could
model the emergence of complex subcultural structures in large populations. In his 1958 book, *The Psychology of Interpersonal Relations*, Fritz
Heider offered what he called *balance theory*.[20] A cultural application of
balance theory would be the observation that people tend to harmonize
their social ties and their cultural orientations. If Person A is friends with
Person B and Person B is committed to Politics X, then Person A may
tend to adopt Politics X as well. However, if Person A is already committed to Politics Y, then there is an imbalance. It can be solved by Person
A adopting Person B's politics, Person B adopting Person A's politics, or
the two people breaking off their friendship. My 1987 book and software collection, *Sociology Laboratory*, included a rule-based simulation
combining Sutherland and Heider, but also a far more cognitive neural net simulation charting the social discovery and sharing of religious
compensators.[21] Here I will rerun a much more recent version using the
multiagent rule-based software I developed for my 2006 book, *God from
the Machine: Artificial Intelligence Models of Religious Cognition*, focusing
on the Sutherland–Heider theory.[22]

Cyburg is a town of exactly 44,100, living in one-person homes
arranged as a square 210 on a side. Obviously, this is an abstraction, and
the number 44,100 was selected not only because it was a good size for
simulations of this kind, but also a perfect square evenly divisible by all
integers, 1 through 7, plus 9, 10, 12, 14, 15, 20, 25, 50, and 100. Each
person (except those unfortunate enough to have a home on the edge of
town) had eight neighbors, with each of whom a friend relationship could
exist. The software offered a graphics display of little colored squares, with
lines representing the friendships, and as the computer ran the colors

---

[20]   Heider, F. 1958. *The Psychology of Interpersonal Relations*. New York: Wiley.

[21]   Bainbridge, W.S. 1987. *Sociology Laboratory*. Belmont, California: Wadsworth.

[22]   Bainbridge, W.S. 2006. *God from the Machine: Artificial Intelligence Models of
Religious Cognition*. Walnut Grove, California: AltaMira.

could change and lines could appear and disappear. The colors gave a visual impression of the competing subcultures, but after each run in which each of the 44,100 has a chance to act, a table of data could be opened giving the current census of group membership.

The software gave the opportunity to make many choices for a given run of the simulation, allowing subsequent comparison of results from different preconditions. For the one run reported here, in Table 4.1, the first decision was that there should be five approximately equal subcultures in Cyburg—call them religious cults—so the simulation began by giving each resident in turn a one-fifth chance of starting in each subcult. The Sutherland and Heider theories were given equal probability of being applied by each simulated person on each turn. Under Sutherland's differential association theory, the simulated person would keep or adopt the

Table 4.1 Simulation of competing cults with different outreach cultures

Turn	1.0 Cult	0.8 Cult	0.6 Cult	0.4 Cult	0.2 Cult	Density
0	19.85%	20.12%	20.17%	19.80%	20.05%	50.07%
1	20.28%	20.51%	20.30%	19.42%	19.49%	63.56%
2	21.39%	20.85%	20.12%	19.06%	18.58%	70.36%
3	22.08%	21.42%	20.13%	18.71%	17.66%	74.67%
4	22.96%	21.87%	20.13%	18.24%	16.79%	78.17%
5	23.87%	22.27%	19.90%	17.90%	16.07%	80.45%
6	24.52%	22.58%	19.79%	17.59%	15.52%	82.55%
7	25.21%	22.87%	19.72%	17.30%	14.91%	84.16%
8	25.83%	23.05%	19.65%	16.97%	14.50%	85.30%
9	26.37%	23.21%	19.55%	16.71%	14.16%	86.22%
10	26.75%	23.37%	19.44%	16.56%	13.88%	87.06%
15	28.21%	23.83%	19.24%	15.89%	12.83%	89.35%
20	29.03%	24.18%	19.07%	15.51%	12.21%	90.68%
25	29.45%	24.41%	19.06%	15.29%	11.79%	91.38%
30	29.79%	24.58%	19.00%	15.13%	11.50%	91.65%
35	30.02%	24.73%	19.01%	15.03%	11.22%	91.98%
40	30.21%	24.83%	18.95%	14.95%	11.05%	92.15%
45	30.29%	24.90%	18.96%	14.95%	10.90%	92.27%
50	30.34%	24.95%	18.97%	14.94%	10.79%	92.50%

majority cult membership among friends. The Heider theory was applied just to the friendships, adding ties to members of the same cult, and removing ties to members of other cults. On a modern desktop computer the 44,100 actions of one turn took a few seconds, and 50 turns were run.

Why was the first cult able to grow from 19.85 percent of the population up to 30.34 percent? Because the cultures of the cults were set differently at the beginning of this simulation run. An additional opportunity was given to each simulated person to develop a friendship with a neighbor, regardless of that neighbor's cult membership. That was the outreach and recruitment feature of the Lofland–Stark model, in which members of a cult became deployable agents for it. Members of the most successful cult would always engage in outreach; thus it is called the 1.0 Cult. In the 0.8 Cult, members had just an 80 percent chance of reaching out on a given turn. The cult that shank most in members, from 20.05 percent of the population to 10.79 percent, was the 0.2 Cult with just a 20 percent outreach chance.

This not only illustrates how additional rules can be added to a rule-based simulation, but also how they can be used to analyze the effect of the existing rules. I ran the simulation twice more, once with Sutherland's theory operating all the time, and Heider's not at all, and the other time with only Heider's in effect. The results were similar to each other in that the populations of the groups changed hardly at all, in contrast to Table 4.1. Thus, the Sutherland and Heider factors were both necessary to model competition between subcultures, and outreach was a factor that would increase their differential effect. An important secondary effect was that the density of the social network—the fraction of possible social binds that actually exist—increased from 50.07 percent to 92.50 percent, a strengthening of social structure that would have many consequences had it been experienced by real people.

Simulation of Societal Ideologies

As illustrated by *Neverwinter* in Chapter 2, massively multiplayer online games are art forms that converge movies and literature with artificial social intelligence. Occasionally, their designers incorporate sophisticated social theories, and here the best example is *Fallen Earth*, which depicts the emergence of a collection of competing utopian communities, in the wake of a devastating world war. A reviewer of the manuscript of this book offered a better summary of this section than I had written: "The complex cultures produced in some MMOs allow researchers to play through possible social relations. That playthrough might help them conceptualize their conventional problems differently and might help them rethink how group affiliation works."

To provide the cultural background, Table 4.2 begins by listing four rather famous MMOs that emphasized living in an imaginary environment based on rich ideas, but that no longer exist: *Star Wars Galaxies* (2003–11), *City of Heroes* (2004–11), *Tabula Rasa* (2007–09), and *WildStar* (2014–18). *Star Wars Galaxies* was set in galactic history right after the original *Star Wars* movie, but the action is separated from the main story line of the movies, and emphasized building homes and communities in collaboration with other players. *City of Heroes* drew upon the

Table 4.2 Computer games that simulated complex cultures

Name	Launch date	Wikipedia pageviews	Metacritic professionals		Metacritic user scores	
			Metascore	Critics	Mean	Raters
Multiplayer extinct:						
Star Wars Galaxies	2003	477,201	71	33	5.8	104
City of Heroes	2004	520,194	85	58	8.4	112
Tabula Rasa	2007	143,255	78	34	7.7	111
WildStar	2014	298,112	82	52	7.5	951
Solo player:						
Fallout	1997	1,680,778	89	12	8.8	1,045
Fallout 2	1998	926,374	86	15	9.1	1,187
Fallout 3	2008	2,515,470	91	48	7.8	3,966
Fallout New Vegas	2010	2,021,109	84	39	8.7	3,513
Fallout 4	2015	7,646,883	84	38	5.5	8,124
Multiplayer surviving:						
Fallen Earth	2009	43,844	71	11	6.9	163

established super-hero genre of comics and movies, but chiefly explored and dwelled within a marvelously huge city with a diversity of neighborhoods. *Tabula Rasa* imagined that a few human beings have escaped Earth after aliens conquered our world, and are desperately setting up colonies on two distant planets, interacting with extraterrestrial cultures including the relics of an advanced civilization that had completed scientific discovery. *WildStar*, like a few other MMOs but giving more emphasis to building a home and economy, contrasted two forms of society, anarchic rebels competing with religious imperialists.

The relatively high rating for *City of Heroes* reflects the fact that many people wish it still existed. Ordinary videogames and computer games produced years ago can be played today, merely using the software the player had purchased, but that is not true for massively multiplayer online games, because they require server-based software and a database maintained by the company that published them. Back in 2010, the computer science magazine, *Communications of the ACM*, had published an essay written by my avatar, Rumilisoun, who spoke to readers from Elrond's Library in *Lord of the Rings Online*, a game that has survived:

> The library where I work in Rivendell is 1,000 years old, and I have trouble imagining all the difficulties you might face if you were to try to build a Digital Library of Virtual Worlds. Yet what a shame it would be if the glorious creativity of the first generations of virtual worlds were truly gone forever. The first great grand opera, l'Orfeo, composed by Claudio Monteverdi in 1607 is still performed today, and anyone may buy a recording for a few dollars. Four hundred years from now, I hope your descendants will still be able to visit me so I can introduce them to Frodo, Bilbo, and Gandalf ... and perhaps all go Orc hunting together."[23]

In 2019, a frenzy of communications in gamer forums and blogsites rejoiced when the world discovered that several groups had resurrected versions of *City of Heroes*, triggering active debate about how they could

---

[23]   Rumilisoun. 2010. "Rebirth of Worlds." *Communications of the ACM* 53, no. 12, p. 127.

become legal, given that the company that closed the virtual city down still held the intellectual property rights and how they could adapt to changing technological standards.[24]

Table 4.2 shows the number of pageviews of Wikipedia articles about these virtual worlds, data beginning July 1, 2015, and ending February 1, 2019. These are considerable numbers of views, given that the first three MMOs had shut down before Wikipedia began tabulating views on their pages. Table 4.2 also reports Metacritic data, the metascores which Metacritic calculates through a secret algorithm from the various ratings given by professional critics, and the user scores on a quite different scale. After these four MMOs, we see data for a sequence of five postapocalyptic solo-player games set in various parts of the United States, as the *Fallout* summary article with 4,466,003 pageviews explains:

> The series is set in a fictionalized United States in an alternate history scenario that diverges from reality following World War II. In this alternative atompunk "golden age", a bizarre socio-technological status quo emerges, in which advanced robots, nuclear-powered cars, directed-energy weapons, and other futuristic technologies are seen alongside 1950s-era computers and televisions ... More than a hundred years before the start of the series, an energy crisis emerged caused by the depletion of petroleum reserves, leading to a period called the "Resource Wars" in April 2052—a series of events which included a war between the European Commonwealth and the Middle East, the disbanding of the United Nations, the U.S. annexation of Canada, and a Chinese invasion and subsequent military occupation of Alaska coupled with their release of the "New Plague" that devastated the American mainland. These eventually culminated in the "Great War" on the morning of October 23, 2077, eastern standard time, a two-hour nuclear exchange on an apocalyptic scale, which subse-

---

[24]   massivelyop.com/2019/06/30/the-daily-grind-two-months-in-have-you-tried-the-resurrected-city-of-heroes

quently created the post-apocalyptic United States, the setting of the *Fallout* world.[25]

The fundamental *Fallout* principle has the quality of prophecy: Faith was misplaced that a New World Order would unify humanity in peace and prosperity. Once the world disintegrated, following the principle enunciated by Frederic Thrasher in his 1927 book, *The Gang*, large-scale social disorganization triggered small-scale social organization.[26] Numerous gangs and social movements emerged in distributed locations, each focused on a person or an idea. The independent MMO, *Fallen Earth*, is frequently compared with *Fallout*, and more than once I have seen players discuss the comparisons in the *Fallen Earth* game chat. However, the diffuse postapocalyptic subculture contains many other influential examples, such as the movies *Things to Come* (1936), *On the Beach* (1959), *Mad Max* (1979), and more recently *Divergent* (2014) that also had utopian characteristics. Wikipedia provides this background:

> The *Fallen Earth* story begins in the 21st Century, when the first in a series of natural disasters hits the United States. As Americans struggle to recover, an investment tycoon named Brenhauer buys a controlling stake in a mega-corporation named GlobalTech. By 2051, he moves his headquarters to the Grand Canyon Province, where GlobalTech eventually creates a self-sufficient economic and military mini-state. Meanwhile, in India and Pakistan, the Shiva virus, named for the dance-like convulsions that it caused in its victims, appears among the human populace. As the infection starts to spread, countries accuse each other of engineering the virus. Political paranoia turns to open aggression and nuclear conflict. The nuclear conflict combined with the virus devastates the planet. Less than one percent of Earth's population survived the Fall, and the Hoover Dam Garrison and Grand Canyon Province are the only known outposts of human civilization. Outside the protective confines of the Hoover Dam Garrison, the player

---

[25]   en.wikipedia.org/wiki/Fallout_(series)

[26]   Thrasher, F.M. 1927. *The Gang*. Chicago: University of Chicago Press.

encounters ruins of the old world, genetically altered creatures, strange technology, and six warring factions. Some factions seek to rebuild the old world, others wish to build a new one in their own image, and some simply desire chaos and anarchy.[27]

As described on *Fallen Earth*'s website, although many story-based quest arcs are available, the emphasis is on freedom:

> Explore, harvest and stake your claim to over 1,000 square kilometers of harsh and mysterious terrain. The classless advancement and non-linear gameplay allows you to play the character you want ... Fallen Earth gives you the freedom to do exactly as you want. The world may be a shadow of its former self, but there's no limit to what's possible for you to accomplish.[28]

Each of the "six warring factions" has a coherent, competing utopian ideology, and a major goal of my several periods of research inside *Fallen Earth* was to document their thinking. In an online guide, William Usher explained:

> You do have the option of playing in a neutral organization within the game, but the tradeoff is a depth versus breadth experience. Neutrals can experience a lot more in the game since they aren't being targeted by an enemy faction, while engaging in a faction provides a richer, deeper play experience as players explore the inner politics, specialized Knowledges and community bonds of playing Fallen Earth in a group.[29]

Table 4.3 reports the "reputation" status of each of my four avatars. Bridgebain was my main avatar that represented myself and fully explored this virtual world, while the others offered different perspectives

---

[27] en.wikipedia.org/wiki/Fallen_Earth

[28] www.gamersfirst.com/fallenearth

[29] Usher, W. "Fallen Earth Faction Guide." www.alteredgamer.com/fallen-earth/49916-intro-game-guide-the-factions

based on the thinking of authors whose identities I temporarily adopted. Oswald Spengler was famous for predicting the fall of western civilization.[30] Pitirim Sorokin, founder of the Sociology Department at Harvard, offered a more complex theory in which a culture arose in ideational (ideological) mode, then transformed into sensate (sensual) mode before falling.[31] Mary Shelly suggested in her novel *Frankenstein* that harmful technologies could degrade humanity. The three alt (alternate) avatars halted exploration when they had completed exploring the social groups situated in the Plateau region, where all avatars begin and become familiar with the factions, and Northfields, where their faction membership consolidates.

Table 4.3 serves multiple functions. First, it is the basis for charting the social structure comprised of factions that inhabit this virtual world. Second, it suggests the concepts the factions represent, each a subculture within a larger system that is rather coherent. Third, the very different numbers in the four columns illustrate how people may choose different paths within a multicultural system, combining political and artistic principles in somewhat personal ways. Each column of data could be conceptualized as the responses to a questionnaire from an individual person, although based on behavioral data rather than opinions. The gross structure of the factions arranges them in three categories: (1) the six factions to which both nonplayer characters and the avatars of players belong, (2) four nonplayer factions with which avatars may develop positive reputations, and (3) a number of low-culture gangs of enemies. The reputation scores for the first two groups are somewhat abstract and can be gained in complex ways, the negative scores representing enemy status, meaning that an NPC in the faction would attack the player's avatar if it came near. The scores for the potentially hostile nonplayer factions simply tabulate how many members of each the avatar has killed, with the minus sign emphasizing enemy status.

Originally, the six joinable factions were arranged in a complex system of three pairs of arch-enemies, with each faction having two potential

---

[30] Spengler, O. 1926–1928. *The Decline of the West*. New York, NY: A. A. Knopf.
[31] Sorokin, P.A. 1937–1941. *Social and Cultural Dynamics*. New York, NY: American Book Company.

Table 4.3 Faction reputations of four survivors of world war

Faction	Cultural value	Bridgebain Level 55	Spengler Level 20	Shelley Level 20	Sorokin Level 30
Factions which players may join:					
Lightbearers	Spirituality	6,513	–50,260	27,773	–1,537
Vistas	Balance	82,085	–84,373	0	–2,950
CHOTA	Anarchy	4,950	–42,896	0	–2,009
Travelers	Profit	–13,026	25,126	–55,563	–1,503
Techs	Technology	–164,190	42,184	0	0
Enforcers	Order	–9,900	21,448	0	–2,001
Friendly nonplayer factions:					
Townspersons	Protection	11,309	1,176	1,125	1,244
Bankers	Finance	18,782	1,800	2,300	19,287
Franklin's Riders	Delivery	30,280	6,780	5,530	6,250
Shiva's Favored	Pollution	17,564	0	0	0
Hostile nonplayer factions:					
Clerics of Gates	Cybercultism	–323	–73	–84	–62
Gully Dogs	Raiding	–114	–47	–116	0
Blade Dancers	Violence	–151	–331	–283	–24
Shiva's Blessed-Favored	Pollution	–372	–47	–24	–61
Human League	Purity	–149	–3	–3	–124
Devil's Own	Evil	–462	–66	–83	–277
Gaunt's Raiders	Looting	–116	–99	–13	0
Night Wolves	Thievery	–95	–44	–78	0
Judges	Zeal	–304	–74	–38	–62
White Crows	Russia	–255	–24	–17	–5

allies and two potential enemy factions as well. However, in 2012 this system was simplified, to become just three hostile pairs without alliances connecting some factions.[32] As described in the wiki devoted to *Fallen Earth*, the arch-enemy pairs are Children of the Apocalypse (CHOTA) versus Enforcers, Lightbearers versus Travelers, and Techs versus Vistas:[33]

- The CHOTA are a defiant heretical group who vehemently oppose order.
- The Enforcers are the militaristic body of Fallen Earth. They are based upon strict values of organization and control, and despise anything chaotic or unorganized.
- The Lightbearers are a group of spiritual sages who are dedicated to the practice of martial arts and enlightenment.
- The Travelers are the gypsies of the new world. They travel from place to place, peddling their wares, trying to make as much money as possible.
- The Techs are a group of scientists and engineers who are primarily interested in restoring the world as it once was through technological knowledge.
- The Vistas are advocates of the natural ecosystem.

Originally, there were nine *starter towns* in the Plateau region, locations where avatars could begin their adventures in Fallen Earth, but the number was reduced to three, the other six remaining as places low-level avatars could visit. This major shift represents a common problem for MMOs, but also illustrates a more general challenge faced by subcultures and social movements in the real world. Given great publicity, a new MMO will begin with a flood of players, all of course at level one of experience, who will need room to perform their early missions without getting in each other's way. That requires multiple starter locations, to spread the surge out. But it is also important for new players to encounter other new players, at first cooperating spontaneously, then forming guilds to enable enduring collaboration. Therefore, after the initial surge, a smaller number of starter locations is appropriate. In a study of the

---

[32] "Faction Changes!." January 20, 2012, fallenearth.gamersfirst.com/2012/01/faction-changes.html

[33] fallenearth.fandom.com/wiki/Factions

Transcendental Meditation movement, Daniel Jackson and I observed a flood of new members who trained to become teachers, but the rate of recruitment of newcomers was not sufficient to keep them busy in that prestigious role.[34] Thus the population dynamics of multiplayer games may, at least abstractly, offer insights into evolutions of social structures more generally.

Of the three current starter towns, Boneclaw is dominated by members of CHOTA, and the emphasis is on teaching combat skills to new avatars. Given their anarchistic tendencies, the CHOTA of Boneclaw are rather disorganized, with low morale and partly divided into subfactions. By completing several quests, the player can unify the CHOTA of the town, but this does not give the player's avatar an improved reputation with CHOTA, because faction affiliation does not begin until the second main region, Northfields. The Midway starter town is dominated by Travelers, and the training emphasis is on crafting, which makes sense because the travelers are merchants and crafting produces products that may be sold. Like the CHOTA of Boneclaw, the Travelers of Midway are divided, but into the equivalent of two competing crime families, and one quest has the player select which of the two family leaders to murder, also not gaining faction reputation. The third starter town, Clinton Farm, emphasizes support missions and does not have a dominant faction.

The six other original starter towns were similarly arranged in two trios, in each of which one town specialized in teaching combat, crafting, or support. Mumford was the crash site of a radioactive military satellite and remains conflict-oriented, as the wiki page for its missions reports:

> You have a choice to either support Jon Dawkins and the Vistas with cleaning up the radioactive waste from the Mumford Crash Site or supporting Mercury Reynolds and the Techs with salvaging the valuable technology. The rewards do vary based on which side

[34] Bainbridge, W.S., and D.H. Jackson. 1981. "The Rise and Decline of Transcendental Meditation." in *The Social Impact of New Religious Movements*, ed. B. Wilson, 135–158. New York, NY: Rose of Sharon.

you support, but supporting one side or the other plays no part in your eventual faction alliance.[35]

Nearby South Burb belongs to the Vistas, has flourishing farms, and emphasizes crafting, while North Burb belongs to the Lightbearers and is the region's main center for production of medical supplies. In the third triad of starter zones, Zanesville belongs to the Enforcers and emphasizes combat; Depot 66 belongs to the Travelers who teach crafting and have set up a Shakespeare theater, and Terance where several missions involve a ruined LifeNet facility and an insane artificial intelligence named TETRAX.

Upon returning to *Fallen Earth* to complete the research for this section, I created my fourth avatar, naming her Mary Shelly after the author of *Frankenstein*, and deciding she should emphasize medical training, become a Lightbearer, which required her to be an enemy of the Travelers, and unlike the three other avatars avoid entanglement in any of the other four primary factions. She stayed for a while in North Burb, doing as many Lightbearer missions as she could, and marveling at what she learned. In an online guide to the factions, William Usher wrote:

> The Lightbearers are wandering disciples who teach peace and emphasize spiritual, mental and physical development. They believe in protecting their "light" within and fighting for peace if necessary. They follow the teaching of Shakti, a woman who traveled the Province healing and protecting the innocent in the years after the fall, and excel in martial arts and close combat techniques.[36]

Wikipedia reminds us:

> Shakti ... is the primordial cosmic energy and represents the dynamic forces that are thought to move through the entire uni-

---

[35]   fallenearth.fandom.com/wiki/Mumford_Missions

[36]   Usher, W. "Fallen Earth Faction Guide." www.alteredgamer.com/fallen-earth/49916-intro-game-guide-the-factions

verse in Hinduism and Shaktism. Shakti is the concept or person-ification of divine feminine creative power, sometimes referred to as "The Great Divine Mother" in Hinduism.[37]

Thus, we might conclude that the Lightbearers are adherents of Hinduism. However, the main architectural feature of North Burb is a pagoda, a kind of structure more fully developed in China and Japan, where martial arts are especially traditional. Just east of the pagoda, Mary Shelly found Master Henry Solomon sitting in an eastern meditative pose, prepared to teach her not only martial arts but also self-mastery. His proclamation of faith superficially suggests an Asian religion:

> In the spirit of our ancestors, we pride ourselves in harmony of body, spirit, and mind. Through our body, we connect ourselves to the earth, taking what we need from it, and giving back that which the earth requires. Through our spirit, we connect with one another, forming a community of life that weathers the greatest of storms. Through our mind, we connect to ourselves, becom-ing honest to our abilities and the true meaning of our existence. Wisdom lies not in the mastering of the mind, but the combined strength of body, spirit, and mind.[38]

However, that proclamation really came from a very different source, Luther Halsey Gulick Jr. (1865–1918), "an American physical educa-tion instructor, international basketball official, and founder with his wife of the Camp Fire Girls, an international youth organization now known as Camp Fire."[39] I knew this because I and my sister had attended two of the summer camps he founded in Maine, Timanous, and Little Wohelo, where everybody sang, "He has welded a symbol, Body, Spirit, and Mind"—sung to the melody of the first "Pomp and Circumstance" march by Sir Edward Elgar.[40] The Timanous symbol is a triangle that has

---

[37]   en.wikipedia.org/wiki/Shakti
[38]   fallenearth.fandom.com/wiki/Mission:_Mastering_One%27s_Self
[39]   en.wikipedia.org/wiki/Luther_Gulick_(physician)
[40]   en.wikipedia.org/wiki/Camp_Timanous; camptimanous.com; wohelo.com

also played a role as the symbol of the Young Men's Christian Association (YMCA), and an outline of its history states,

> Luther H. Gulick, who revolutionized sports and physical fitness at the YMCA, proposed a red equilateral triangle as a symbol in 1891. It was adopted immediately by Springfield College. The sides of the triangle, Gulick said, stood for "an essential unity: spirit, mind, and body: each being a necessary and eternal part of man."[41]

In a history of the college, Laurence Doggett described Gulick as "a combination of virility with a great deal of the theoretical" and speculated he might have derived the triad from Buddhism.[42] However, his source of the idea that Buddhism was trinitarian was a 1940 tourism book, but not a scholarly study, and the mystique of a trinity is certainly central to Christianity.[43]

At the risk of unleashing endless theological debates, we might speculate that: Jehovah = mind; Christ = body; the Holy Spirit = spirit. In much earlier centuries, wars were fought between the Homoousions and the Homoiousians, who disagreed literally by one iota of difference over whether Christ was the same as God or merely similar.[44] Perhaps in the Age of Artificial Intelligence there will be similar bloodletting over the exact identity of the Holy Spirit. Gulick was not a partisan in such debates and gave *spirit* a far different meaning, close to *joy*:

> When I speak of the "higher life of the spirit," do not apprehend that we are drifting into a religious discussion. A higher *liveliness* of the spirit would have expressed my thought even more adequately. The "play of the spirit" is not an empty phrase. It is always the spirit that plays. Our bodies only work. The spirit at

---

[41]   www.greenbayymca.org/about/history/history-of-the-ymca-logo

[42]   Doggett, L.L. 1943. *Man and a School.* New York, NY: Association Press.

[43]   Forman, H. 1940. *Horizon Hunter*, 147. New York, Robert M. McBride and Company.

[44]   en.wikipedia.org/wiki/Homoousion; en.wikipedia.org/wiki/Homoiousian

play is what I mean by the higher life. Play is the pursuit of ideals. When released from the daily work, the mill we have to tread in order to live, then we strive to become what we would be if we could. When we are free we pursue those ideals which indicate and create character. If they lead us toward wholesome things—literature, music, art, debate, golf, tennis, horseback riding and all of the other things that are wholesome and good, then our lives are rounded out, balanced and significant.[45]

Within the universe of massively multiplayer online games, *Fallen Earth* has sufficient verbiage and intellectual content to be considered literature or philosophical debate, but its spiritual play element is also achieved by the horseback riding Gulick mentioned, indeed the riding of many different steeds and vehicles. His profound comment, "Play is the pursuit of ideals" may describe many of the subcultures explored in this book, not merely the Lightbearers.

My four *Fallen Earth* avatars never debated the contrasting merit of the factions, but chose four very different paths for themselves, as four different players might have done, thus illustrating multiperspective phenomenology conducted by a single researcher. Bridgebain was the original explorer, entering the virtual world December 30, 2011, at a time when there were six available starter towns, of which he selected Clinton F.A.R.M., aware it was under siege by the Blade Dancer gang and that it was not really a *farm* but a school for "Fire, Alpine Rescue and Medical." Initially, he aligned himself with the two more nonviolent and spiritual factions, by experience level 23 reaching a reputation score of 43,914 with the Vistas and 36,230 with the Lightbearers. As an experiment, on May 8, 2012, he obtained a Faction Reset potion from an NPC named Disgruntled Outsider and erased all six of his main faction reputations. In his first phase of research, the unified system of factions was enforced by the software, but he continued to follow that structure after it became optional, in part because many of the quests had been designed on the basis of the original faction structure. When he completed exploration

---

[45]   Gulick, L.H. 1909. "Popular Recreation and Public Morality." The *Annals of the American Academy of Political and Social Science* 34, no. 1, pp. 33–42, 33–34.

of the entire territory and reached the experience cap of level 55, he had positive reputations with three factions: Techs (187,594), Travelers (174,542), and Enforcers (75,686).

A new research project reset Bridgebain's reputations again, so he could explore the environmentalist Vista faction more thoroughly, and two more avatars were added, Spengler and Sorokin, based on two theorists of the decline of civilization, Oswald Spengler and Pitirim Sorokin.[46] Spengler reached level 20 without doing any crafting, while Sorokin reached 20 without unnecessarily killing any human NPCs. For this new research in 2019, Sorokin's affiliations with the six main factions were reset, and he decided he would oppose all of them. Meanwhile, Mary Shelley constantly affiliated with the Lightbearers as she ascended the experience levels. Unlike some of the most popular virtual worlds, *Fallen Earth* does not record how many hours each avatar has been played, but the total for this study was certainly more than 300 hours and more likely 400. MMO players often are active in a particular game in a series of episodes, as illustrated by the periods I operated one or more of the four avatars: December 2011 to April 2012, December 2012 to March 2013, August to September 2013, August to September 2014, January to February 2019. This complex history suggests how real people in the real world may affiliate intermittently with subcultures over the course of their lives.

Conclusion

Computer simulations have always seemed to me to be an efficient but also creative way to explore the meaning of social theories, and thus today very applicable to cultural science. By "always" I mean since I obtained a Geniac "computer" in 1956, the educational system designed by Edmund C. Berkeley, a founder of the Association for Computing Machinery. As Wikipedia recalls: "Widely advertised in magazines such as *Galaxy Science Fiction*, the Geniac provided many youths with their first hands-on

---

[46]   Spengler, O. 1926–1928. *The Decline of the West*. New York: A.A. Knopf; Sorokin, P.A. 1937–1941. *Social and Cultural Dynamics*. New York: American Book Company.

introduction to computer concepts and Boolean logic."[47] At that point I had read every monthly issue of *Galaxy* since it was first published in 1950 and was especially impressed by Alfred Bester's novel *The Demolished Man*, which had been serialized in *Galaxy* in 1952, and was the first novel to win the prestigious Hugo award.[48] Decades later, when Bester and I were both panelists at a science fiction convention, I jokingly praised him for having invented a new religion, but really his novel was a deep exploration of social-psychological theory, assuming the existence of telepathy in order to explore some of the deep implications of psychoanalysis. After his death in 1987, it was fascinating to see him simulated as a character revealingly named Bester, in the *Babylon 5* television science fiction series.[49] What can we today learn by telepathically reading Bester's mind? Fiction, whether in the form of traditional printed literature, television programs, or computer games, is the most extensive simulation of human reality. Thus, the main topic of literature studies in the humanities has always been mental simulations of human experience, today largely published through computers.

---

[47] en.wikipedia.org/wiki/Geniac
[48] en.wikipedia.org/wiki/The_Demolished_Man
[49] en.wikipedia.org/wiki/Alfred_Bester_(Babylon_5)

CHAPTER 5

Revolutionary Revaluation of Literature

Arts and entertainment are highly valuable industries that also serve many humane functions, such as encouraging introspection about ethical questions, the relations humans have with each other, and the wider meaning of an individual life. For the past several centuries, even as publication technologies evolved substantially, there has persisted a distinction between the "high culture" supported by wealthy donors and taught in university humanities courses, and popular culture sold to the supposedly unsophisticated "masses." This distinction may be obsolete, as well as invidious, but it points to a currently crucial fact: much "high culture," such as the plays of Shakespeare and the novels of Dickens, is currently in the public domain, while distribution of "pop culture" products is restricted by intellectual property rights. Should copyrights be eternal or cease to exist? Is it possible to imagine a best-selling mystery concerning a murderer sinisterly named Graves, who kills authors, because "writing down of words is considered to be too sacred an act to be profaned by ordinary every-day uses?"[1] I must admit having plagiarized that idea from a novel by Robert Graves, but why should anybody write new fiction, when the classics of literature are far too extensive for anyone to complete reading in a lifetime? Conversely, why should college professors teach classes about the literature of the past, when millions of works of fiction are published online each year? Dan Cohen, the vice provost for information collaboration at Northeastern University, reports: "University libraries around the world are seeing precipitous declines in the use of

---

[1] en.wikipedia.org/wiki/Seven_Days_in_New_Crete

the books on their shelves."[2] The profession of writing and the industry of literature publishing may always have been in constant turmoil, but the obsolescence of the printing press will have great implications for their futures.

The Semiprofessional Tradition in Literature

The uncertain states of literature creation and cultivation illustrate the problematic status of culture in modern economies. Should writing be limited to a small fraction of the population who are professionals in this craft? Or is story-telling a talent shared by many people, such that like other arts it should be decommercialized? In recent centuries, mass publication of literature has become a major industry and the precursor to technology-based artforms such as movies and multiplayer online role-playing games. Yet many of the most famous authors were unable to earn a living in that line of work. Emily Brontë was not a professional author when she penned *Wuthering Heights*, and Jane Austen's struggle to earn meager income by writing six novels is well known, but their difficult situations were not limited to English female writers of two centuries ago.[3] A trio of socially connected fantasy-horror geniuses of the 1930s illustrate the morbid turns of fate.

The Wikipedia page for H.P. Lovecraft, which was viewed 5,896,141 times from July 1, 2015, through April 11, 2019, reports: "He was virtually unknown during his lifetime and published only in pulp magazines before he died in poverty, but he is now regarded as one of the most significant 20th-century authors of horror and weird fiction."[4] Robert E. Howard, author of the *Conan* stories, committed suicide at the age of 30, and "His greatest success occurred after his death."[5] That success consisted not merely in the reprinting of the stories he wrote about Conan the Bar-

---

[2] Cohen, D. 2019. "The Books of College Libraries Are Turning Into Wallpaper." *The Atlantic*, May 26, 2019, www.theatlantic.com/ideas/archive/2019/05/college-students-arent-checking-out-books/590305/

[3] en.wikipedia.org/wiki/Emily_Brontë; en.wikipedia.org/wiki/Jane_Austen

[4] en.wikipedia.org/wiki/H._P._Lovecraft

[5] en.wikipedia.org/wiki/Robert_E._Howard

barian, but the continuation of the mythos by other writers, successful movies in which his character was played by the actual future governor of California, successful computer games, and 887,665 pageviews. A. Merritt, with only 53,411 pageviews, is less well known today, but he "made $25,000 per year by 1919, and at the end of his life was earning $100,000 yearly—exceptional sums for the period."[6] But Merritt made his living as a very successful journalist and editor, not for the high quality of his fiction writing. Personally, I consider his 1924 novel *The Ship of Ishtar* to be a great work of literature, rich in metaphor and philosophy as well as action, and I added the page about it to Wikipedia, but it gained only 9,889 pageviews during the same recent period.[7]

An entire book could be filled with similar examples, but as a general rule most authors of literature begin as amateurs, survive as semiprofessionals, and only a few really gain fame and wealth through their writing. Today the role-model is J.K. Rowling, as suggested by her 13,361,958 pageviews, author of the *Harry Potter* fantasy series on which many successful movies have been made:

> Rowling has lived a "rags to riches" life story, in which she progressed from living on state benefits to being the world's first billionaire author. She lost her billionaire status after giving away much of her earnings to charity, but remains one of the wealthiest people in the world.[8]

As it happens, I have published one novel, earning exactly $2,000 from it, and four other members of my immediate family have published novels, thus providing a *participant observation* basis for research using less personal methods. The birth of Internet, and automatic methods for printing paper books, may be changing the economic context for literature, but we cannot yet be sure in which ways, given the chaotic experience of authors of the past.

---

6   en.wikipedia.org/wiki/A._Merritt
7   en.wikipedia.org/wiki/The_Ship_of_Ishtar
8   en.wikipedia.org/wiki/J._K._Rowling

A more systematic basis for looking forward can be gained by looking backward at the most influential periodical of the so-called Golden Age of Science Fiction, a magazine founded in 1930 as *Astounding Stories of Super-Science* but surviving today as *Analog Science Fiction and Fact*. Primarily remembered as *Astounding Science Fiction*, it was the core of the SF subculture of authors, readers, and author-readers in the period 1937 to 1971 under the editorship of John W. Campbell, Jr.[9] Each issue of the magazine began with an editorial, included a nonfiction article on a topic relevant to science fiction, and ended with a section of letters from readers, but the main content was stories and serialized novels. I published six articles in *Analog* myself, three of them around the year 1980 and three around 2000.[10] Campbell's editorial in the April 1938 issue proclaimed:

> A magazine is not an autocracy, as readers tend to believe, ruled arbitrarily by an editor's opinions. It is a democracy by the readers' votes, the editor serving as election board official. The authors are the candidates, their style and stories their platform.

With these words he defined the function of a monthly reader poll called the Analytical Laboratory that ran from March 1938 through October 1976. Each "AnLab" summarized readers' ratings of the stories from a previous issue, thus a precursor of modern recommender systems.

The data for 464 issues covering about 2,500 fiction items provided popularity ranking for a vast number of authors, 53 of whom had published at least 10 items—short stories, novelettes, or installments of serialized novels. Here, Table 5.1 summarizes the data for the 13 highest ranking authors, stopping with Isaac Asimov, perhaps the best known

---

9   en.wikipedia.org/wiki/Analog_Science_Fiction_and_Fact

10   Bainbridge, W.S., and M. Dalziel. 1978. "New Maps of Science Fiction." *Analog Yearbook* 1, pp. 277–299; Bainbridge, W.S., and R. Wyckoff. 1979. "American Enthusiasm for Spaceflight." *Analog* 99, no. 7, pp. 59–72; Bainbridge, W.S. 1980. "The Analytical Laboratory, 1938–1976." *Analog* 100, no. 1, pp. 121–134; Bainbridge, W.S. 2000. "The First Martians." *Analog* 120, no. 7, pp. 81–89; Bainbridge, W.S. 2001. "The Poverty of Nations." *Analog* 121, no. 3, pp. 47–56; Bainbridge, W.S. 2002. "A Question of Immortality." *Analog* 122, no. 5, pp. 40–49.

Table 5.1 Reader ratings of authors from the analytical laboratory

Author's name	Stories rated	Mean date	Reader ratings		Wikipedia pageviews
			Place	Points	
Anson MacDonald	10	1941	210	98	
Robert A. Heinlein	25	1947	228	145	1,723,155
E.E. "Doc" Smith	13	1944	244	190	116,702
Jerry Pournelle	11	1973	280	265	295,654
A.E. van Vogt	59	1944	348	298	185,943
Harry Harrison	32	1966	321	316	206,796
Lawrence O'Donnell	11	1947	330	323	
Frank Herbert	28	1963	381	329	811,656
Poul Anderson	67	1960	348	332	272,777
Hal Clement	29	1953	315	340	45,657
Jack Williamson	19	1944	348	343	78,634
Clifford D. Simak	39	1949	356	350	134,719
Isaac Asimov	45	1950	391	351	4,266,782

of the 53 today. AnLab listed the authors and story titles from the given recent issue in descending order, beginning with the story in first *place*, but also reporting a *points* score that Campbell calculated from the sets of rankings in the letters he received from readers. In a factual science article published in the 50th anniversary issue of the magazine, I reported statistical methods for combining the place and points scores from issues that contained different numbers of fiction items.[11] Those two forms of reader ratings are given in Table 5.1, recalibrated in terms of a scale from 1 (best—a hypothetical author whose works would always be rated better than works by other authors) to 1,000 (worst).

The table appears to list 13 authors, but in a sense there are only 11, but perhaps really 13. Anson MacDonald was a penname used by Robert A. Heinlein, and Anson was his full middle name. Lawrence O'Donnell was also a penname, but for a married couple, Henry Kuttner and C.L. (Catherine Lucille) Moore. The table includes Wikipedia pageviews from

---

[11]   Bainbridge, W.S. 1980. "The Analytical Laboratory, 1938–1976." *Analog* 100, no. 1, pp. 121–134.

July 1, 2015, through April 10, 2019, indicating that Heinlein and Asimov have remained popular, along with Frank Herbert who wrote the *Dune* series of novels that developed into a popular multimedia subculture. The fact that Lawrence O'Donnell did not exist might not prevent him from having a Wikipedia page, because there is one for a different penname used by the same couple, Lewis Padgett which had 19,694 pageviews, and the individual members of the couple have pages, Henry Kuttner with 77,770 pageviews and C.L. Moore with 68,911.

Wikipedia correctly reports that Heinlein was considered the "dean of science fiction writers" and a leader in the hard-science SF tradition that expected authors to provide cogent technical explanations for any unusual phenomena and to explore possible future technologies. Yet, Wikipedia also notes: "His work sometimes had controversial aspects, such as plural marriage in *The Moon is a Harsh Mistress*, militarism in *Starship Troopers* and technologically competent women characters that were strong and independent, yet often stereotypically feminine."[12] Actually, as I read his works they all had politically controversial aspects, sometimes right-wing, sometimes authoritarian, sometimes libertarian, sometimes anarchist, sometimes radical but difficult to define. Indeed, he explored many different ways in which a community of people could organize themselves, even as he was also exploring the implications of spaceflight and related technologies. Today, Heinlein's thinking can be explored by joining Facebook groups that discuss his works, such as:

Heinlein Forum (2,356 members): "For fans of Robert A. Heinlein, the first Grand Master of Science Fiction. Little is off topic, but no copyright infringement allowed or encouraged. Specialization is for Insects."

Heinleiners (1,135 members): "A community where people with Robert Heinlein in common can discuss whatever the hell they choose... who will take responsibility for their own feelings, and

---

[12] en.wikipedia.org/wiki/Robert_A._Heinlein

who LIKE intelligent discussion, especially with people who dis-agree with them. Like the original RAH."

Apostles of Heinlein (748 members): "This group was begun as a place of joy and sharing; it is for people to discuss All Things Heinlein: the ideas, inventions, and social structures Heinlein cre-ated in his works, both fiction and non-fiction. This is what has brought us all together here."

Heinlein was a rare example of financial success in writing, but most of the others on the list were part-time authors. E.E. Smith is considered the father of *space opera*, "a subgenre of science fiction that emphasizes space warfare, melodramatic adventure, interplanetary battles, chivalric romance, and risk-taking."[13] The *Star Wars* saga is the most familiar exam-ple of space opera, a term derived from analogy with *soap opera* and more directly the Wild West stories called *horse opera*. Yet Smith's main source of income was his prosaic work as a "food engineer (specializing in dough-nut and pastry mixes)."[14] Rather more integrated in his work, Jerry Pour-nelle held a number of responsible positions in the aerospace industry.[15]

A.E. van Vogt illustrates the connection between a genre of literature and a set of radical intellectual movements that seek to apply the same imagination to the real world. He was

always interested in the idea of all-encompassing systems of knowl-edge (akin to modern meta-systems)—the characters in his very first story used a system called "Nexialism" to analyze the alien's behavior. Around this time, he became particularly interested in the general semantics of Alfred Korzybski. He subsequently wrote a novel merging these overarching themes, *The World of Ā*, originally serialized in *Astounding* in 1945. Ā (often rendered as Null-A), or non-Aristotelian logic, refers to the capacity for, and

---

[13]   en.wikipedia.org/wiki/Space_opera

[14]   en.wikipedia.org/wiki/E._E._Smith

[15]   en.wikipedia.org/wiki/Jerry_Pournelle

practice of, using intuitive, inductive reasoning (compare fuzzy logic), rather than reflexive, or conditioned, deductive reasoning.[16]

A sense of the radical ambitions of the General Semantics movement can be gleaned from the titles of Korzybski's two main publications, *Manhood of Humanity* and *Science and Sanity*.[17] For a while van Vogt partnered with another *Astounding* author, L.R. Hubbard, in setting up an unconventional psychotherapy movement, Dianetics, which Hubbard later transformed into the religion named Scientology.[18] Hubbard first announced Dianetics in a nonfiction article in *Astounding*; as a fiction author, he was in 30th place among the 53 prolific AnLab authors, stressing action and psychology in his stories, rather than technical accuracy. In stark contrast, Hal Clement was a teacher of chemistry and astronomy at Milton Academy, a conventional Massachusetts boarding school, and wrote technically careful novels about the environments of realistic but exotic planets.[19]

Rather than summarize how the other authors found various ways to support their writing, we should conclude this section with consideration of Isaac Asimov. Like Clement, he taught science in Massachusetts, specifically being a professor of biochemistry at Boston University.[20] Much of

---

[16] en.wikipedia.org/wiki/A._E._van_Vogt

[17] Bainbridge, W.S. 1994. "General Semantics." In *The Encyclopedia of Language and Linguistics*, eds. R.E. Asher and J.M.Y. Simpson, 1361. Oxford: Pergamon

[18] Bainbridge, W.S., and R. Stark. 1980. "Scientology: To Be Perfectly Clear." *Sociological Analysis* 41, pp. 128–136; Bainbridge, W.S. 1987. "Science and Religion: The Case of Scientology." In *The Future of New Religious Movements*, 59–79. eds. D.G. Bromley and P.E. Hammond. Macon, Georgia: Mercer University Press; Bainbridge, W.S., and R. Stark. 2001. "Scientology." In *Concise Encyclopedia of Language and Religion*, eds. J.F.A. Sawyer and J.M.Y. Simpson. Oxford, United Kingdom: Pergamon Press; Bainbridge, W.S., and R. Stark. 2005. "Scientology." In *The Encyclopedia of Religion and Nature*, eds. B. Taylor, 1499–1500. London, Thoemmes Continuum; Bainbridge, W.S., and R. Stark. 2009. "The Cultural Context of Scientology." In *Scientology*, eds. J.R. Lewis, 35–51. New York: Oxford University Press.

[19] en.wikipedia.org/wiki/Hal_Clement

[20] en.wikipedia.org/wiki/Isaac_Asimov

his significant financial success as an author came from his prolific writing of factual science books and articles aimed at the general public. Two profound but not necessarily unique ideas provided powerful intellectual focus for much of his influential fiction: (1) The Foundation and (2) the three laws of robotics. The Wikipedia article for Asimov's *Foundation* received 2,140,800 pageviews and offers a correct summary:

> The premise of the series is that the mathematician Hari Seldon spent his life developing a branch of mathematics known as psychohistory, a concept of mathematical sociology. Using the laws of mass action, it can predict the future, but only on a large scale. Seldon foresees the imminent fall of the Galactic Empire, which encompasses the entire Milky Way, and a dark age lasting 30,000 years before a second great empire arises. Seldon's calculations also show there is a way to limit this interregnum to just one thousand years. To ensure the more favorable outcome and reduce human misery during the intervening period, Seldon creates the Foundation—a group of talented artisans and engineers positioned at the twinned extreme ends of the galaxy—to preserve and expand on humanity's collective knowledge, and thus become the foundation for the accelerated resurgence of this new galactic empire.[21]

Asimov reported that his idea came from reading *The Decline and Fall of the Roman Empire* by Edward Gibbon, but at the time he wrote his original *Foundation* trilogy in the 1940s, several influential intellectuals had written about the possibility that our own civilization like ancient Rome might soon collapse. Notable among them were Oswald Spengler and Pitirim Sorokin, but also Jacob Moreno who argued in 1934 that some new form of sociology might prevent this disaster.[22] In the New World Order after the fall of the Soviet Union, optimism held sway for a couple of decades in our real world, but today we have renewed concern that civilization may be inching toward its demise. Where is Hari Seldon

[21] en.wikipedia.org/wiki/Foundation_series
[22] Moreno, J.L. 1934. *Who Shall Survive?*. Washington, D.C.: Nervous and Mental Disease Publishing Company.

when we need him? Also today, there is much discussion of the pros and cons of artificial intelligence, and renewed interest in the three laws of robotics that Asimov offered:

1. A robot may not injure a human being or, through inaction, allow a human being to come to harm.
2. A robot must obey the orders given it by human beings except where such orders would conflict with the First Law.
3. A robot must protect its own existence as long as such protection does not conflict with the First or Second Laws.[23]

Originally published in *Astounding* in a 1942 story named "Runaround," and most prominently republished in Asimov's 1950 anthology, *I, Robot*, the laws were presented as somewhat problematic.[24] Much of Asimov's extensive robot fiction concerns situations in which algorithms come into conflict, either with each other or with the surrounding real world, and often considering the algorithms that govern human rather than robot behavior. Today, major computer science organizations promulgate recently improved systems of ethics, but they may be ineffective in ways that Asimov could have used as the basis of many new stories. Most obviously, in the application of elaborate systems in a complex world, how can algorithms predict what actions may cause harm, and to what extent? The literature of past centuries can illuminate today's issues, not by answering questions but by raising them. In 2019, the National Science Foundation partnered with the Amazon corporation "to jointly support computational research focused on fairness in AI, with the goal of contributing to trustworthy AI systems that are readily accepted and deployed to tackle grand challenges facing society."[25] Yet the local newspaper in Amazon's home city raised questions about the company's objectivity, and we may well imagine Asimov writing a fascinating novel about

---

[23] en.wikipedia.org/wiki/Three_Laws_of_Robotics
[24] Bainbridge, W.S. 1986. *Dimensions of Science Fiction*, 73. Cambridge, Massachusetts: Harvard University Press.
[25] www.nsf.gov/pubs/2019/nsf19571/nsf19571.htm

a corporation that seeks to impose ethics algorithms on society that will serve its own interests.[26]

A Local Science Fiction Fandom

A sense of how we can study a subculture through its people rather than its products can be gained by looking on Facebook, starting with a group representing one of the most established science fiction clubs, the New England Science Fiction Association, familiarly known as NESFA, pronounced "NESS-fuh." Science fiction fans originally assembled around the magazines, which included letter-to-the-editor sections and encouraged social networks to emerge. Indeed, participants tended to be comfortable with the term "fan," despite the implication that fans are *fanatics* who overvalue the object of their admiration. They used the term in unusual ways, for example, giving *fan* the plural *fen* rather than *fans*, analogous with *man* and *men*. A controversial proverb emerged: "Fans are slans." This makes sense only to fen who loved the 1946 novel *Slan* by A.E. van Vogt, the early activist in the Dianetics movement that was a predecessor of Scientology which aims to transcend traditional human limitations. Wikipedia explains:

> Slans are evolved humans, named after their alleged creator, Samuel Lann. They have the psychic abilities to read minds and are super-intelligent. They possess near limitless stamina, "nerves of steel," and superior strength and speed. When Slans are ill or seriously injured, they go into a healing trance automatically.[27]

Fans called their community *fandom*.

A decisive step in the development of fandom was the first Worldcon—World Science Fiction Convention—where 200 fans and authors

---

[26] Romano, B. 2019. "Amazon's Role in Co-Sponsoring Research on Fairness in AI Draws Mixed Reaction." *The Seattle Times*, March 31, 2019, www.seattletimes.com/business/amazon/amazons-role-in-co-sponsoring-research-on-fairness-in-a-i-draws-mixed-reaction

[27] en.wikipedia.org/wiki/Slan

gathered in the future-oriented 1939 World's Fair in New York.[28] Already, factions battled over the definition of science fiction, and a group of authors with left-wing utopian aspirations called The Futurians was excluded from participation.[29] Since then, fandom has tended to avoid political activism, even though a good fraction of the literature is either critical of current social institutions or explicitly utopian in suggesting radical alternatives.

A regional convention was held in Boston in 1941, named Boskone when we might have expected Boscon: "The name is a reference to the classic Lensman series by E. E. Smith, in which 'Boskone' is a council of villains, and also a name for their civilization."[30] It was organized by a short-lived group, ended with the 1945 meeting, then was revived in 1965 by the equally short-lived Boston Science Fiction Society. Around 1950, students at the Massachusetts Institute of Technology founded the MIT Science Fiction Society which influenced several cultural developments over the years and currently operates a huge SF library. Members were instrumental in founding the Boston Science Fiction Society which included nonstudents and then its successor NESFA in 1967.[31] A more detailed history that includes information about many of the specific authors and fans involved in these groups can be found on a specialized wiki named Fancyclopedia.[32]

In 1973, 74 members of NESFA were kind enough to complete a questionnaire that was a pilot study for the research I did at the 1978 Worldcon.[33] On December 23, 2018, I found that 601 identifiable people belonged to its Facebook group and explored what other groups in

[28] en.wikipedia.org/wiki/1st_World_Science_Fiction_Convention
[29] Moskowitz, S. 1974. *The Immortal Storm*. Westport, Connecticut: Hyperion; Pohl, F. 1978. *The Way The Future Was*. New York, NY: Ballantine; Kyle, D. "SaM - Fan Forever." www.jophan.org/mimosa/m21/kyle.htm; en.wikipedia.org/wiki/Futurians
[30] en.wikipedia.org/wiki/Boskone
[31] en.wikipedia.org/wiki/MIT_Science_Fiction_Society; en.wikipedia.org/wiki/New_England_Science_Fiction_Association
[32] fancyclopedia.wikidot.com/fancyclopedia-3
[33] Bainbridge, W.S. 1986. *Dimensions of Science Fiction*. Cambridge: Harvard University Press.

Table 5.2 A linked set of science fiction Facebook groups

Group	Founded	Admins	Members	NESFAns	Links
New England Science Fiction Association	2008	11	601	601	100.0%
Boskone	2008	8	905	256	42.6%
Fans of Arisia (Unofficial)	2008	3	1,735	150	25.0%
Analog Science Fiction and Fact Magazine Fan Club	2009	1	3,626	103	17.1%
Science Fiction and Fantasy Authors	2008	2	8,384	59	9.8%
ASIMOV'S Science Fiction	2012	3	2,901	44	7.3%
The Harlan Ellison Facebook Fan Club	2007	3	2,797	38	6.3%
Science Fiction Book Club	2010	3	4,674	32	5.3%
Los Angeles Science Fantasy Society	2007	5	1,365	24	4.0%
ERBzine	2012	1	4,665	23	3.8%
Tom Corbett, Space Cadet	2015	2	1,122	12	2.0%
The Dune Saga	2007	6	9,795	9	1.5%
Heinleiners	2016	2	914	6	1.0%

the general science fiction subculture they tended to belong to. Again, interlock analysis can help us see the social structure of a subculture, and this one proves to be diffuse, with a very wide range of connection strengths. Table 5.2 gives the results, based on "scraping" the membership and admin (administrator) lists from 13 groups and assembling them in a spreadsheet. All of them are *public groups*, for which the membership lists are visible to anyone. Facebook has two other kinds of groups. The membership lists and even postings for *closed groups* may not be seen without joining the group, and *secret groups* cannot even be discovered in a search. Of the 601 NESFA members, 35 belong to at least 4 of the other groups, and the average is 1.26. The table arranges the groups in descending order of their interlock percentage with NESFA.

Since 1968, Boskone has been organized by NESFA, so it makes sense that many members of the Facebook group for NESFA also belong to the one for Boskone: 256 of 601 or 42.6 percent.[34] Since 1990, another SF con has been held annually in the Boston area, named Arisia.[35] Wikipedia tells the world how it relates to Boskone:

> Arisia is a Boston-area, volunteer run science fiction convention, named for a planet in the Lensman novels by E. E. "Doc" Smith. The name was chosen in response to an older Boston-area con, Boskone, which took the typical ending for a convention—con— and then altered the spelling to match the name of an organiza- tion in the Lensmen books.[36]

The Facebook page for the Analog Science Fiction and Fact Magazine Fan Club describes the magazine that is its focus:

> Astounding/Analog (often all-encompassingly just called ASF) is often considered the magazine where science fiction grew up. When editor John W. Campbell took over in 1938, he brought to Astounding an unprecedented insistence on placing equal empha- sis on both words of "science fiction." No longer satisfied with gadgetry and action per se, Campbell demanded that his writers try to think out how science and technology might really develop in the future—and, most importantly, how those changes would affect the lives of human beings. The new sophistication soon made Astounding the undisputed leader in the field, and Camp- bell began to think the old title was too "sensational" to reflect what the magazine was actually doing. He chose "Analog" in part because he thought of each story as an "analog simulation" of a possible future, and in part because of the close analogy he saw

---

[34]   www.nesfa.org/boskone-history/boskone-history.html

[35]   www.arisia.org/AboutArisia

[36]   en.wikipedia.org/wiki/Arisia

between the imagined science in the stories he was publishing and the real science being done in laboratories around the world.[37]

While correct, this paragraph does not emphasize the fact that Campbell and some of his authors hoped that some controversial theories might prove to be true, thus expanding the definition of science to cover what was often disparaged as pseudoscience. Both *Slan* and *The World of Null-A* were originally published in *Astounding Science-Fiction*, and L. Ron Hubbard published supposedly factual science articles there to promote Dianetics in 1950 and 1951, prior to expanding this psychotherapy into the religion of Scientology. In 1956 Campbell himself published about psionics, the development of electronic devices to detect paranormal phenomena such as telepathy. A theme lurking in all chapters of this book is the question of how far science can and should be developed.[38]

The Facebook group Science Fiction and Fantasy Authors is one of a large set of groups that primarily serve people who want to become authors in a particular genre and are sharing hopes and advice. Of its 8,384 identifiable members, 59 also belong to the NESFA group, which is 9.8 percent of NESFA but only 0.7 percent of SFFA. Its self-description says it is:

A group of fiction writers focused on discussing the genres of Science Fiction and Fantasy and springboarding the genres into mainstream literature. This group is open for anyone who loves the genres of Science Fiction and Fantasy. We welcome readers, writers, viewers and all lovers of the genres... If we work hard to discuss the genres and build this site I believe we will all become better writers. Better writers mean more Great Science Fiction and Fantasy stories. Good luck all.[39]

---

[37]   www.facebook.com/groups/AnalogScienceFiction
[38]   Gardner, M. 1957. *Fads and Fallacies in the Name of Science*. New York, NY: Dover.
[39]   www.facebook.com/groups/239793746052181

Reading what members have posted reveals them to be thoughtful, creative, and willing to share ideas, but also facing the difficult challenge of how to publish their fiction in a way that is rewarding, whether in monetary terms or at least in social recognition of their work. A common topic is self-publishing, including the computer-based print on demand method, contrasted with finding a commercial publisher that is both reliable and willing to publish a novel by a new author.

The messages posted by members are naturally arranged in chronological order, with the newest message at the top. An alternative is to enter a search term into the Facebook group's discussion, such as *lulu*, which is the name of a company that offers self-publishing services, with this vision: "Lulu offers you the expertise, independence and flexibility to create, buy and share what you love with the world. We are passionate about providing a remarkable experience for you to tell stories, share knowledge and fulfill your creative potential."[40] Searching for "lulu" immediately suggested other search terms, because many of the messages compared different self-publishing alternatives: "I created a lulu account to see what I could do about getting books in print at a lower cost than createspace." "I'm thinking of switching to LULU Publishing. Has anyone worked with them before? What are your impressions? I just don't like Kindle Direct Publishing. They are too big and it's really hard to get support." "As of today... my 90 day exclusive ebook distro with Amazon's KDP Select ended, so I jumped right into Lulu and already have the ebook version on Lulu's sales site and am pending approval for Nook and the Apple market." "Any idea which is best method to get into paperback? Lulu or Amazon? Need to link up paperback distribution and kindle, and other formats... bit of a loss. Next book will be self published."

The other rows of Table 5.2 concern groups related to a variety of aspects of the wider science fiction subculture. ASIMOV'S Science Fiction is comparable to the Analog group, connecting to a magazine published since 1977 and symbolically oriented toward fiction like that written by Isaac Asimov. The Harlan Ellison Facebook Fan Club is "a group for people on Facebook who are fans and friends of award winning

---

40   www.lulu.com/about/our-story

author, screenwriter, media and social critic, and Grand Master in multiple literary fields, Harlan Ellison (1934–2018)."[41] The Science Fiction Book Club observes: "In the old days, book clubs were informal gatherings where people got together to discuss a common book they were reading. With the advent of the Internet, it's possible to discuss books online."[42] Comparable to NESFA, the Los Angeles Science Fantasy Society, "founded October 27, 1934, is this world's oldest continuously-active science-fiction and fantasy club."[43]

Probably the most extensive nonprofit organization dedicated to the work of an individual American SF writer is the multidecade, multiform fandom currently represented by ERBzine, the "Official Edgar Rice Burroughs Tribute and Weekly Webzine Site Since 1996 ~ 15,000 Web Pages in Archive."[44] It connects to an older manifestation:

> The Burroughs Bibliophiles is a nonprofit 501c(3) literary society devoted to studying and promoting interest in the works, creations, and life of Edgar Rice Burroughs, including the globally popular icon, Tarzan®. The Burroughs Bibliophiles was founded on 4 Sep 1960 and adopted "The Burroughs Bulletin" journal, the only such publication personally approved by Edgar Rice Burroughs.[45]

The *Bulletin* had been founded in 1947, originally as a mimeographed *fanzine*, the standard SF term for fan magazine.[46] The Dune Saga concerns the series of novels, almost like a 1960s' variant of the Mars novels by Burroughs, by Frank Herbert and successor authors, that was first published in *Analog*, while as we already saw Heinleiners concerns Robert A. Heinlein who also published in *Analog*, but mainly in the 1940s.

---

[41]   www.facebook.com/groups/4586629500

[42]   www.facebook.com/groups/130411676997908

[43]   www.lasfsinc.info///index.php?option=com_content&task=view&id=9&Itemid=357

[44]   www.erbzine.com/

[45]   www.burroughsbibliophiles.com

[46]   www.burroughsbibliophiles.com/burroughs_bulletin.html

The Tom Corbett, Space Cadet group is dedicated to a children's television program of the same name that ran from 1950 through 1955. As Wikipedia documents, two of the actors that played main characters became prolific authors, Frankie Thomas who was the eponymous Tom Corbett, and Jan Merlin who played his cranky radio operator, Roger Manning.[47] The origins of the show are complex:

> Joseph Greene of Grosset & Dunlap developed Tom Corbett, Space Cadet, inspired by the Robert A. Heinlein novel Space Cadet (1948) but based on his own prior work. Greene had submitted a radio script for "Tom Ranger" and the "Space Cadets" on January 16, 1946, but it remained unperformed when Heinlein's novel was published.[48]

A website named Solar Guard that launched in 1996 has preserved the history of this classic TV sci-fi series as well as *Space Patrol* that was first broadcast six months before *Tom Corbett*.[49] The main actor in *Space Patrol*, Ed Kemmer, had been a fighter pilot during the Second World War, was shot down over France, and held in a prisoner of war camp for nearly a year.[50] Thus, in reality he was very much like the science fiction character that he played, and his life story suggests that both *Tom Corbett* and *Space Patrol* were in part inspired by technological advances in the real-world conflict that raged immediately before television became a popular culture medium.

The example of Ed Kemmer, a man who actually lived for a time in a technological context like the one he later role-played in a fictional TV series, reminds us that the relationship between culture and truth is complex. It may be true that members of culture X believe statement Y to be true, but objectively Y is false. Statistical studies of a society may find that belief Y has a moderately strong positive correlation with belief Z, but that may result because a large subculture associates Y positively

---

[47] en.wikipedia.org/wiki/Frankie_Thomas; en.wikipedia.org/wiki/Jan_Merlin

[48] en.wikipedia.org/wiki/Tom_Corbett,_Space_Cadet

[49] www.solarguard.com

[50] en.wikipedia.org/wiki/Ed_Kemmer

with Z, while a smaller subculture associates Y negatively with Z. Or, a small correlation may result simply because the data collection method is flawed, and considerable noise hides the power of a strong correlation. In a remarkably detailed summary of extensive research literature, Alexandra Olteanu, Carlos Castillo, Fernando Diaz, and Emre Kiciman have documented a huge array of problems using statistical methods to analyze data concerning online social media.[51] They do not prove that such research is useless, merely that both the phenomena under study, and the research methods, are complex and must not be misunderstood as providing clear and definitive results.

The perspective taken by this book is that statistical research methods have many applications, and rigorous testing of precisely defined formal hypotheses is only one of them. Anomalies may be interesting discoveries rather than research flaws. The human brain evolved under environmental and social conditions that are very different from those experienced by people today. Sociologist Satoshi Kanazawa has made this point in the Savanna Principle, named after the complex East African ecosystem that combined woodland and grassland where humanity evolved, which he has expressed in two different ways:

1. A hypothesis about human behavior fails to the extent that its scope conditions and assumptions are inconsistent with what existed in the ancestral environment.[52]
2. The human brain has difficulty comprehending and dealing with entities and situations that did not exist in the ancestral environment.[53]

---

[51] Olteanu, A., C. Castillo, F. Diaz, and E. Kiciman. 2017. "Social Data: Biases, Methodological Pitfalls, and Ethical Boundaries." *Social Science Research Network*, March 29, 2017, papers.ssrn.com/sol3/papers.cfm?abstract_id=2886526

[52] Kanazawa, S. 2004. "The Savanna Principle." *Managerial and Decision Economics* 25, no. 1, pp. 41–54.

[53] Kanazawa, S. 2009. "Evolutionary Psychological Foundations of Civil Wars." *The Journal of Politics* 71, no. 1, pp. 25–34.

Online social media are very different from our historical homeland, and one consequence is that users may invest it with a great variety of meanings, rendering it a suitable environment for a diversity of subcultures. In a sense, traditional cultural anthropology was respectfully seeking to understand exotic cultures from the standpoint of 20th-century European culture, as a corrective for colonialism but also an extension of it. We may today seek to think beyond our own cultural limits, but research like this book will inevitably have some of the quality of intellectual tourism in which members of one culture visit another culture and seek to understand it. Quantitative research methods can be very useful for providing a set of wider and deeper perspectives that go beyond merely looking out the window of a tour bus, as well as mapping both the internal structure of a culture and its connections to neighboring cultures. Thus here we will tend to use statistics as tools for description rather than hypothesis-testing, although one result will be many new hypotheses that have some empirical confirmation, within the particular cultural context.

Online Fan Fiction

Fandoms are subcultures that not only allow members of an audience to share their enthusiasm for a genre or franchise, but also communities that can support their own members' creative activities. As of April 14, 2019, the online amateur literature digital library, Archive of Our Own, contained 32 stories that mention Asimov's three laws of robotics.[54] This was a tiny fraction of the approximately 4,714,000 works accessible through the site, and some of the 32 mentioned robots only in passing. But some of them would be of value to a cultural scientist who was seeking to map the heritage of the three laws. A story by Zaylo titled "IRobot" quotes the three laws in its summary, along with this:

> Based on the song "IRobot" By Jon Bellion, Keith is a robot created by the company Widget, made to serve humankind as slaves and assistants. Widgets are made to be emotionless, but Keith is

---

[54]   archiveofourown.org/tags/Three%20Laws%20of%20Robotics/works

different, and his feeling will drag him through love and heart-break as he learns how to be a human.

Jon Bellion is a real life "rapper, singer, songwriter and record pro-ducer" whose Wikipedia article has 1,813,246 pageviews.[55] His song "iRobot" is a lament from an apparently rejected lover who has been stripped of his humanity and now requires only "circuits and wires":

I am a robot, thoughtless and empty

Don't know who sent me, don't know who made me

Electric robot, everything's gray now

Numb to the pain now, I knew what love was...[56]

Conceptualizing humanity as possessing transcendent feelings, rather than mechanistically governed by algorithms, is certainly not a new idea. We see it in the 1816 short story "The Sandman" by E.T.A. Hoffmann about love for a clockwork woman that was retold in the ballet *Coppélia* by Léo Delibes and the opera *Les Contes d'Hoffmann* by Jacques Offen-bach.[57] The word *robot* was introduced into literature in the 1920 play *R. U. R.* by Karel Čapek, in which it served as a political metaphor for the dehumanization of the working class, a theme also central to the 1927 movie *Metropolis*.[58] The 1900 novel *The Wonderful Wizard of Oz* by L. Frank Baum includes the Tin Woodman, a worker who had lost most of his humanity to the point of rusting solid. Dorothy cures his paralysis technologically by oiling his joints, and he asks: "Do you suppose Oz could give me a heart?" She replies, "Why, I guess so... it would be as easy as to give the Scarecrow brains."[59] Perhaps ironically, the title "I, Robot" was not original with Asimov, but used in 1939 by the first in a series of popular science fiction stories by Eando Binder about Adam Link, a

---

[55] en.wikipedia.org/wiki/Jon_Bellion

[56] genius.com/Jon-bellion-irobot-lyrics

[57] en.wikipedia.org/wiki/The_Sandman_(short_story)

[58]   en.wikipedia.org/wiki/R.U.R.;   en.wikipedia.org/wiki/Metropolis_(1927_film)

[59] Baum, L.F. 1900. *The Wonderful Wizard of Oz*, 56. Chicago: Hill.

robot that seeks to become human. The author was not exactly a person, also, being the collaboration between two brothers, Earl Andrew Binder and Otto Oscar Binder (Eando Binder = E and O Binder). In summarizing the Adam Link stories in an earlier publication, I described their beginning:

> this metal humanoid with a sponge iridium brain is falsely accused of murdering his creator, Dr. Link. Despite his habit of saving humans from drowning, fires, and auto accidents, he is not exonerated until the third story in the series. Adam Link is strong, intelligent, and especially sensitive. He frequently broods about the sad fate of Frankenstein's monster. People fear Adam at first and later poke fun at him. Continually, he must assert that robots, too, are human. Why, he wonders, cannot people realize, "as Dr. Link once stated, that the body, human or otherwise, is only part of the environment of the mind?"[60]

This debate can be conceptualized as fundamental questions in either cognitive science or cultural science. Can emotions be classified rigorously as distinct categories of cognition? Can the distinction between feeling and thinking be mapped onto different parts of the brain, or are they the contrast between chemical and electronic processes? Is the distinction between human and robot equivalent to the distinction Pitirim Sorokin proposed for cultural science between sensate and ideational culture? Or is it the dimension of variation between multiculturalism and totalitarianism? Other sections of this book gingerly address limited aspects of these cosmic questions, but they certainly cannot be definitively answered here.

However, a television franchise with some of the quality of Asimov's writing has repeatedly compared humans and robots that represent a diversity of emotional and mental archetypes: *Doctor Who*. Things were never exactly what they seem, in the world of the Good Doctor, as illustrated by the fact that his spaceship, named the Tardis, was the size and

---

[60]   Bainbridge, W.S. 1986. *Dimensions of Science Fiction*, 72. Cambridge, Massachusetts: Harvard University Press.

appearance of a police telephone booth. Today, a wiki named Tardis illustrates how it could be bigger on the inside than the outside by containing fully 71,380 articles. One concerns robots called K9,

> the designation given to a series of intelligent, dog-like robots who served as companions of Professor Marius, the Fourth Doctor, Leela, Romana, the Mistress, Sarah Jane Smith, Luke Smith, Starkey, and the Tenth Doctor. K9 Mark I, II, III, and IV addressed whoever was directing them as "Master" or "Mistress" depending upon gender, and used the formal "affirmative" and "negative" rather than "yes" and "no". They were programmed to be both loyal and logical, with a penchant for taking orders literally, almost to a fault.[61]

So K9 robots were adorable pets, rather than dangerous monsters, in contrast to the robotoid Cybermen and Daleks who were mechanized derivations of biological "people."

Doctor Who is a British television series that began in 1963 and that I first watched when I visited in 1965. Wikipedia offers many pages about it, including one for each of the 13 manifestations of the doctor played by different actors over the years:

> The programme depicts the adventures of a Time Lord called "the Doctor," an extraterrestrial being, to all appearances human, from the planet Gallifrey. The Doctor explores the universe... Accompanied by a number of companions, the Doctor combats a variety of foes while working to save civilisations and help people in need.[62]

Seeking a diversity of viewpoints on canine robots, one can visit the online fan literature digital library, Archive of Our Own, go to the 53,077 stories, chapters, and other works of literature in the *Doctor Who* section, on May 4, 2019, and tell the search engine to list all the stories and other works that include "K9," getting these hits: K9 (106), Sarah Jane

[61] tardis.fandom.com/wiki/K9

[62] en.wikipedia.org/wiki/Doctor_Who

Table 5.3 Amateur literature featuring the 13 Doctors with their companions

Doctors 1–13		1st frequent companion		2nd frequent companion		3rd frequent companion	
Period	Works	Name	Works	Name	Works	Name	Works
1. 1963–66	542	Susan Foreman	211	Ian Chesterton	121	Barbara Wright	116
2. 1966–69	675	Jamie McCrimmon	490	Zoe Heriot	193	Victoria Waterfield	107
3. 1970–74	726	Jo Grant	247	Sarah Jane Smith	123	Liz Shaw	55
4. 1974–81	735	Sarah Jane Smith	307	Romana	173	Harry Sullivan	99
5. 1982–84	806	Tegan Jovanka	253	Nyssa of Traken	228	Vislor Turlough	183
6. 1984–86	479	Peri Brown	174	Evelyn Smythe	53	Melanie Bush	50
7. 1987–89	506	Ace McShane	275	Melanie Bush	36	Bernice Summerfield	22
8. 1996	1,185	Rose Tyler	267	Grace Holloway	85	Chang Lee	12
9. 2005	4,208	Rose Tyler	3,298	Jack Harkness	1,495	Adam Mitchell	43
10. 2005–10	13,089	Rose Tyler	8,925	Jack Harkness	2,809	Donna Noble	2,767
11. 2010–13	9,130	River Song	3,596	Amy Pond	3,245	Rory Williams	2,543
12. 2014–17	5,571	Clara Oswald	3,198	River Song	878	Bill Potts	493
13. 2018–	2,270	Yasmin Khan	1,430	Ryan Sinclair	942	Graham O'Brien	924

Smith (79), K9 (Doctor Who) (66), Jack Harkness (54), Fourth Doctor (52), Rose Tyler (51), Tenth Doctor (50), Romana II (Doctor Who) (48), Mickey Smith (38), Martha Jones (33).[63] Apparently, 52 stories about the Fourth Doctor include K9, as do 50 about the Tenth Doctor and 79 about one of the Doctor's favorite companions, Sarah Jane Smith. The fact that the list includes the circular reference "K9 (Doctor Who)" illustrates that the classification system is complex, and very extensive data preparation work may be required prior to serious study. Table 5.3 is less rigorous, offering an approximate count of the numbers of stories about each of the 13 Doctors and their most popular companions.

The general structure of *Doctor Who* stories is that the current Doctor wanders around the universe, often having adventures in which he picks up a companion, visits one or more planets where the companion shares some adventures, and then leaves the companion somewhere while acquiring another. Multiple companions may overlap with each other, and a companion may overlap two Doctors in the sequence. In the table we see that companion Sarah Jane Smith was in 123 stories with Doctor 3 and 307 stories with Doctor 4, but we would need to look more closely to determine if perhaps all three interacted in some of them. Searching for the trio suggests there were 64 such stories, but given the time travel easily achieved by the Tardis, some of these would tell about the trio interacting simultaneously, while more conventional stories might describe Sarah's experience during the transition between the two Doctors. Thus a table like this one is only an introduction or strategic map, preparing for more detailed research.

Seven Doctors spanned the time period from 1963 to 1989, when the first series stopped. In 1996, a TV movie attempted to revive the series, but failed to achieve that goal. Then in 2005 the Ninth Doctor launched a second series. The numbers of stories building on the second series are far greater than those for the first series, suggesting that the young authors who contributed to Archive of Our Own became interested in *Doctor Who* while watching new broadcast episodes. Rose Tyler was a companion for both Doctor Nine and Doctor Ten, implying that the stories about

---

[63] archiveofourown.org

her with Doctor Eight involve an imagined transition that was never made into television episodes.

Another online digital library comparable to Archive of Our Own is FanFiction.net, where fans published 63,400 items related to *Doctor Who*.[64] A random example would be the most recently updated contribution, the novel by "vaiken" titled Space Oddity, that had this description:

> Rose Tyler had one mission: Don't be discovered. The Doctor has accepted that Rose is forever lost to him. Time and Fate have other plans. Season 4 reunion fic. Rated: Fiction T—English—Romance/Angst—10th Doctor, Rose T. —Chapters: 18—Words: 61,171—Reviews: 46—Favs: 45—Follows: 109—Updated: 58m ago—Published: Jul 16, 2017—id: 12575193."

The reviews, favs, and follows illustrate that FanFiction.net is a social medium, as well as a library, and it includes several *Doctor Who* role-play forums, which are the equivalent of collective-authorship theater dramas. Here are the brief descriptions that introduce the four with the largest number of contributions:

The Man with the Age-Old Eyes
Come here to Roleplay Doctor Who style! Have wild adventures in the TARDIS, and meet all sorts of new people. :P English—Topics: 36—Posts: 92,252—Since: Dec 9, 2012.

Doctor Who Roleplay
A roleplay forum, for all of the Doctors and their companions. OC and crossover friendly. Some roleplays can contain mature themes (violence, assault, death, etc). We are always looking for new members, so please drop in and say hello! Established 2012. English—Topics: 136—Posts: 60,394—Since: Aug 16, 2012.

The TARDIS
Because we're all Whovians here, aren't we? Challenges, games, talks related and unrelated to the DW world. English—Topics: 248—Posts: 47,649—Since: Jun 27, 2010.

---

[64] fanlore.org/wiki/FanFiction.Net

Classic and New Who Roleplay!

> Join the Doctor in his travels through time and space. 6 roleplay top-
> ics: Classic Who RP, New Who RP [FULL], 12th Doctor RP [FULL],
> Alternate Universe (Female Doctor) RP, Long Post RP, Random RP.
> WARNING: Participants may be required to wait after creating a
> character before joining a roleplay topic if they are all mid-plot, as
> characters may only join upon us beginning a new plot. Limited space
> available in each topic. English—Topics: 24—Posts: 35,817—Since:
> Feb 23, 2011.

FanFiction.net has a search feature called *crossover* that allows users to read
stories that combine material from two different sources. Of these *Doctor
Who* works, 12,834 included material from some other source, the two
most common being the 1,697 crossovers with the Sherlock TV series
that updates Sherlock Holmes and 1,203 crossovers with the *Harry Potter*
books and movies, both of which share the Doctor's English origins. In
Chapter 1 we noted the popularity of *Game of Thrones*, a television series
about a fictional land called Westeros that seems rather like medieval
England and where the characters have English accents. It was based upon
the series of novels titled *A Song of Ice and Fire* by George R.R. Martin.
The amateur stories based on these franchises are given descriptive *tags*
when they are published at FanFiction.net. Many are familiar terms, but
at least two are recent: "Angst: A story with an angsty mood centered on a
character/characters who are brooding, sad, or in anguish."

> Hurt/comfort: A story in which a character is put through a trau-
> matizing experience in order to be comforted. The ultimate goal
> of these stories is often to allow for close examination of two char-
> acters' bond with one another and is sometimes seen as a alterna-
> tive to more sexual content.[65]

Table 5.4 shows the distribution of descriptive tags for six popular
traditions of fan literature.

---

[65]   en.wikipedia.org/wiki/Fan_fiction

Table 5.4 Thematic descriptions of fan fiction online publications

Genre	Doctor Who	Harry Potter	Sher-lock	Sherlock Holmes	Game of Thrones	A Song of Ice and Fire
Adventure	8.4%	4.9%	1.9%	5.6%	7.8%	5.5%
Angst	8.1%	7.1%	8.6%	7.1%	5.2%	6.4%
Crime	0.1%	0.2%	1.7%	3.0%	0.3%	0.4%
Drama	6.0%	9.9%	6.6%	7.0%	12.8%	12.8%
Family	2.8%	3.5%	3.9%	1.8%	5.5%	7.7%
Fantasy	0.7%	1.5%	0.4%	0.3%	7.1%	5.3%
Friendship	6.3%	3.8%	9.4%	13.9%	2.7%	3.0%
General	16.6%	17.1%	16.1%	18.3%	15.0%	21.0%
Horror	0.5%	0.6%	0.4%	0.6%	0.6%	0.5%
Humor	9.1%	11.1%	9.9%	9.4%	3.2%	3.1%
Hurt/com-fort	7.4%	3.8%	9.8%	6.2%	6.0%	5.2%
Mystery	1.4%	1.3%	2.7%	10.6%	0.5%	0.6%
Parody	0.5%	1.0%	0.4%	0.9%	0.5%	0.4%
Poetry	0.9%	0.7%	0.4%	1.6%	0.4%	0.4%
Romance	20.1%	30.0%	23.9%	9.5%	28.5%	23.6%
Sci-Fi	7.9%	0.1%	0.2%	0.3%	0.1%	0.2%
Spiritual	0.2%	0.2%	0.1%	0.4%	0.1%	0.2%
Supernatural	0.4%	0.5%	0.8%	1.1%	0.6%	0.6%
Suspense	0.8%	0.6%	1.0%	1.2%	0.8%	0.7%
Tragedy	1.6%	2.0%	1.7%	1.3%	2.1%	2.5%
Western	0.0%	0.0%	0.0%	0.0%	0.0%	0.0%
Total	100.0%	100.0%	100.0%	100.0%	100.0%	100.0%
Total tags	118,435	1,391,637	114,408	7,108	14,016	15,678
Total items	63,400	765,000	59,500	3,900	7,500	8,500

By far the most common tag is *romance*, with the rather mean-ingless *general* in second place. The authors of fanfiction are dis-proportionately female, and researchers have begun studying this very creative subculture, to understand the implications for modern life.[66] The romance tag is rarer for stories based on the traditional Sherlock Holmes culture, rather than the recent Sherlock TV series, and as we might expect, *mystery* is more common than for the other five subcultures. The crucial point of this table is documentation of how numerous and diverse a sample of the fan fiction universe seems to be.

Conclusion

The cultures of contemporary societies are changing rapidly in ways that are little understood. For example, in 1972 the General Social Survey found that 29.1 percent of respondents attended religious services no more frequently than once a year, but that fraction of the population detached from religious organizations had risen to 47.1 percent in 2014.[67] A common theory of what is happening is that science is replacing religion as our source of truth, yet it may instead be that culture is changing in other ways that have yet to be understood or even named.[68] Vocal Atheists seem still to be rare and do not seem to offer moral guidance that was one of religion's traditional functions.[69] Indeed, science itself may face the equivalent of secularization, losing faith and organizational influence, if people have placed too many utopian hopes in it.[70] An alternate model is that many aspects of human culture go through a long-term curvilinear rise and fall, such as demonstrated by family structure that began simple in the Savanna, became very complex in tribal and agricultural societies,

---

[66]   Curtin, M.E. 2000. "The Fan Fiction Universe: Some Statistical Comparisons." September 30, 2000, www.alternateuniverses.com/fanficuniv.html; Fiesler, C., S. Morrison, and A.S. Bruckman. 2016. "A Case Study of Feminist HCI and Values in Design." *Proceedings of CHI'16.* New York: ACM.

[67]   sda.berkeley.edu/sdaweb/analysis/?dataset=gss14, using the unweighted data.

[68]   Gorski, P.S., and A. Altinordu. 2008. "After Secularization?" *Annual Review of Sociology* 34, pp. 55–85; Evans, J.H., and M.S. Evans. 2008. "Religion and Science: Beyond the Epistemological Conflict Narrative." *Annual Review of Sociology* 34, pp. 87–105.

[69]   Amarasingam, A. 2010. *Religion and the New Atheism.*

[70]   Bainbridge, W.S. 2017. *Dynamic Secularization.* London: Springer.

then simplified again in postindustrial societies.[71] Perhaps literature began as verbal storytelling among friends and families, became more elitist when writing was invented, became commercial when paper printing was invented, but now returns to informal storytelling, but online rather than around campfires. If this is true for some arts or genres, we may wonder to what extent this model will describe the future of all. Such developments may have huge economic and social impacts. Whether to guide businesses based on literature or educational classes taught by academics, an active, exploratory, and creative cultural science is sorely needed.

---

[71]   Blumberg, R.L., and R.F. Winch. 1972. "Societal Complexity and Familial Complexity: Evidence for the Curvilinear Hypothesis." *American Journal of Sociology* 77, no. 5, pp. 898–920.

CHAPTER 6

Denotation, Connotation, Transcendence, and Translation

The humanities are of great significance for all the themes explored in this book, and this chapter will document the fact that the forms of artificial intelligence being developed today lack the ability to interpret language as human beings can, especially erudite humanistic scholars. Among the most active areas often considered artificial intelligence is *natural language processing*, in which "natural" specifies the topic as human languages, rather than, for example, computer programming languages.[1] However, natural languages might be defined to include bird songs and wolf howls, predating by many millions of years the evolution of the human species. The current use of speech to communicate and comprehend complex factual situations is a recent development, and originally our voices had different purposes, chiefly to support social solidarity and exchange values. Language evolved in bands comparable to surviving hunter-gather societies studied by some anthropologists, where an inarticulate shout in the forest may alert other members of a hunting team to the location of the shouter, and an infant's cry may have alerted its mother to the need to nurse it. Machine translation was developed to convey complex factual information from a descriptive narrative, but the use of language to communicate complex concepts is a relatively recent *exaptation* from the natural functions of human voice.[2] The relevance today is that language has not lost its original sociobiological functions, even though computer

---

[1] en.wikipedia.org/wiki/Natural_language_processing
[2] Gould, S.J., and E.S. Vrba. 1982. "Exaptation—A Missing Term in the Science of Form." *Paleobiology* 8, no. 1, pp. 4–15.

scientists seem to think it has. They need to realize two things: (1) Some applications of natural language processing will never work reliably, frequently producing invalid results that can be quite costly. (2) Many potential applications of computer and communications technologies to language may prove to be far more valuable and intellectually interesting than computer scientists currently realize.

The Marriage of True Minds

This is not the place to explore deeply the vast literature on human cognition related to language, or the unverified but sincere theories about how human language evolved. Rather, we can start with a simple dichotomous categorization of linguistic functions, *description* versus *expression*: (1) Descriptive use of language conveys information about reality, most reliably concerning conditions in the physical world. (2) Expressive speech, writing, and gesture emphasize the idiosyncratic perceptions and emotions of the individual, in a social context where human-to-human relationships are important. This book includes music among the central topics of cultural science, and its tones and rhythms can be seen as derivations from the expressive forms of spoken language. Songs bridge from speech to music, and it is not difficult to read anger into the words as well as rhythms of a 1950s' popular song: "See you later, alligator. After 'while, crocodile."[3] This is how a man remembers the dismissive words of a girlfriend when she rejects him and starts a romance with another man.[4]

As noted in Chapter 1, some humanist philosophers, notably Alfred Korzybski, founder of the mid-20th century intellectual movement called General Semantics, have raised doubts about the possibility of accurate description, thus preparing us a lifetime later to doubt the feasibility of natural language processing by computers. He asserted this thesis through aphorisms: "the word is not the thing," "the map is not the territory," and even the mathematically radical axiom $A \neq A$. But we should provisionally accept the principle that computers can do a good job searching, interpreting, and translating descriptive text. We already mentioned this

---

[3] en.wikipedia.org/wiki/See_You_Later,_Alligator

[4] genius.com/Bill-haley-and-his-comets-see-you-later-alligator-lyrics

perspective back in Chapter 1, and perhaps it was invented thousands of years ago by Tyrion Lannister, unless, of course, you think that *Game of Thrones* depicts the human future, not our past, given that author George R.R. Martin was originally a science fiction author. An alternative framework for the same idea is cultural relativism, merely noting that the smallest and possibly most fundamental culture is the mind of an individual human being, who will map the world in idiosyncratic ways.

What about the potential for computer applications oriented toward human expression? This chapter will suggest that they can be useful tools to support human judgment, but cannot perform the tasks themselves. Here is an example that may seem trivial—but jokes are a significant form of human expression—that links to an important source of insight. When thinking about how to illustrate the meaning of description, after already having prepared a little text about translation of chemical terms between English and German, this "poem" came to mind:

We had a little Willy,
Now Willy is no more,
For what he thought was H_2O
Was H_2SO_4.

Perhaps Willy felt thirsty. He saw a container of liquid on the laboratory table. He thought it was water, so he drank it. But it was actually sulfuric acid, and it killed him. Clearly, our emotions may sometime lead us astray, and had he known the objective meaning of H_2SO_4 that may have been written on the container's label, he might still be alive today. Wanting to cite this example here, I sought the source of this poem, using Google, but all I initially found was a number of casual comments using different versions of it, with no information about its source. So I adjusted the search to look only inside Google Books and quickly discovered that Susanne K. Langer had quoted it in her 1942 book, *Philosophy in a New Key*, which I recalled having read decades ago and admired.[5] She was a major proponent of scholarship on the humanistic or expressive aspects of

---

[5] Langer, S.K. 1942. *Philosophy in a New Key*, 65. Cambridge, Massachusetts: Harvard University Press.

language, and would today criticize natural language processing from that perspective. Wikipedia offers a good summary of her thinking:

> Langer's philosophy explored the continuous process of meaning-making in the human mind through the power of "seeing" one thing in terms of another. Langer's first major work is entitled, *Philosophy in a New Key*. It put forth an idea that has become commonplace today: that there is a basic and pervasive human need to symbolize, to invent meanings, and to invest meanings in one's world. Beginning with a critique of positivism, the work is a study of human thought progressing from semantic theory through philosophy of music, sketching a theory for all the arts. For Langer, the human mind "is constantly carrying on a process of symbolic transformation of the experiential data that come to it," causing it to be "a veritable fountain of more or less spontaneous ideas."[6]

So, we can imagine that Langer is alive today, sitting at her computer, and playing with Google Translate. She decides to challenge it with a sentence from poetry that exactly raises her favorite issues concerning description versus expression: "Love is not love which alters when it alteration finds, or bends with the remover to remove." Note that it includes the physically descriptive term *bends* and has three pairs of duplicated terms having a variety of linguistic forms. She instructed Google Translate to give her its translation into each of six languages, then told it to give her the back-translation, for example, the English word *love* producing the German word *Liebe*, and the German word *Liebe* giving the English word *love*. Note that in English *love* is either a noun or a verb, while all nouns in German are capitalized, so *Liebe* equals the noun form of *love*, while *liebe* equals the verb form (in first person singular: *ich liebe*). Here are her results:

> German: Liebe ist keine Liebe, die sich verändert, wenn sie Veränderungen findet, oder sich mit dem Entferner verbiegt, um sie zu entfernen.

---

[6] en.wikipedia.org/wiki/Susanne_Langer

Back-translation: Love is not a love that changes when it finds change, or bends with the remover to remove it.

Spanish: El amor no es el amor que se altera cuando encuentra la alteración, o se dobla con el removedor para eliminar.

Back-translation: Love is not love that is altered when it finds the alteration, or is bent with the remover to eliminate.

French: L'amour n'est pas l'amour qui se modifie lorsqu'il trouve altération, ou se penche avec le dissolvant pour le supprimer.

Back-translation: Love is not love that changes when it finds alteration, or leans with the solvent to suppress it.

Hungarian: A szeretet nem olyan szerelem, amely megváltoztatja, amikor megváltozik, vagy elhajlik az eltávolítóval.

Back-translation: Love is not a love that changes when it changes or loses with the remover.

Finnish: Rakkaus ei ole rakkaus, joka muuttaa, kun se muuttuu, tai taivuttaa poistoaineella.

Back-translation: Love is not love that changes when it changes, or bends with a remover.

Lithuanian: Meilė nėra meilė, kuri keičia, kai ji keičia, arba sulenkia su nuėmikliu, kad jis būtų pašalintas.

Back-translation: Love is not a love that changes when it changes or bends with a stripper to remove it.

The German and Spanish back-translations are rather close to the original English, although not exactly the same. But the French version translates *remover* as if it referred to something like paint remover—*solvent*. Similarly the Lithuanian version comes up with *stripper*. How do we know that those translations are incorrect? Because the sentence was quoted from Sonnet 116 by William Shakespeare that begins, "Let me not to the marriage of true minds admit impediments."[7] Shakespeare was very explicitly stating a cognitive perspective on the human meaning of real love, thus exactly relevant to the discussion here. The lines following those we translated clarify further: "O no! it is an ever-fixed mark that looks

---

[7] www.poetryfoundation.org/poems/45106/sonnet-116-let-me-not-to-the-marriage-of-true-minds

on tempests and is never shaken; it is the star to every wand'ring bark, whose worth's unknown, although his height be taken." But what about that word *bark*? Is it a word like "woof" in the canine language? The skin of a tree? No, I believe it is an alternate spelling of *barque* and thus meaning a small sailing ship. The constant reliability of true love is thus a guiding star that gives our lives meaning in the sense of having a direction to go, without necessarily telling us what we will find at our marriage destination.

One tiny perplexity is Shakespeare's use of the word *his*, a masculine pronoun that seems to refer to the star, although modern English would not assign a gender to an astronomical object. This point reminds us that it can be very difficult to distinguish description from expression in many contexts of language use. Furthermore, it is difficult to determine the extent to which languages "think" differently about nonbiological phenomena when they assign nouns to masculine or feminine gender. A starry example is how the sun and moon are named, the two astronomical objects of almost exactly the same visual size but having very different impacts on human life. In Latin, *sol* meaning *sun* is masculine, while *luna* meaning *moon* is feminine. In German, *die Sonne* meaning *the sun* is feminine, while *der Mond* meaning *the moon* is masculine. In ancient days, many natural phenomena were personified, so in recent centuries science may have gradually drained expression from many areas of description, but not completely and not much if at all in the areas central to human emotions and social relations.

A chemical rather than astronomical example returns to the poem about H_2O and H_2SO_4. The page for water in the German-language Wikipedia begins: "Wasser (H_2O) ist eine chemische Verbindung aus den Elementen Sauerstoff (O) und Wasserstoff (H)."[8] *Sauerstoff* clearly translates as *oxygen*, and yet the roots *sauer* and *stoff* imply that the word means *sour stuff*. Similarly, *Wasserstoff* can mean *hydrogen* or *water stuff*. The reason oxygen was conceptualized as sour stuff was an error early in the history of modern chemistry, as reported by the English-language Wikipedia:

---

[8] de.wikipedia.org/wiki/Wasser

Lavoisier renamed "vital air" to oxygène in 1777 from the Greek roots ὀξύς (oxys) (acid, literally "sharp", from the taste of acids) and -γενής (-genēs) (producer, literally begetter), because he mistakenly believed that oxygen was a constituent of all acids. Chemists (such as Sir Humphry Davy in 1812) eventually determined that Lavoisier was wrong in this regard (hydrogen forms the basis for acid chemistry), but by then the name was too well established.[9]

English-speakers are unlikely to know the etymology of *oxygen*, while German-speakers will be aware of the connotation of *Sauerstoff*, illustrating again the possibility that descriptions of natural phenomena in different languages will have connotations, whether significantly or insignificantly shaping human cognition.

In an article for a linguistics encyclopedia, I noted:

Our understanding of the world is powerfully shaped by science, and science expresses itself through distinctive terminology. Although science has the most modern vocabulary, it draws heavily upon dead languages. Intended to provide an unambiguous, exact picture of reality, it may at times inhibit insight and distort communications through its choice of words. Each science has its own linguistic character, and the division between the natural and social sciences is as great as any that separates language families.[10]

Two examples I explored in depth were paleontology and the social sciences. Paleontology and both botany and zoology of contemporary organisms have relied heavily upon the Linnaean taxonomy that assumed that living organisms were naturally organized into a tree diagram of strictly separated categories: kingdom, phylum, class, order, family, genus, and species. In Chapter 3 we noted that this system was historically based on the assumption that God created the species to be distinct sets of living

---

[9] en.wikipedia.org/wiki/Oxygen

[10] Bainbridge, W.S. 1994. "Scientific Nomenclature." In *The Encyclopedia of Language and Linguistics*, eds. R. E. Asher, 3685–3690, 3685. Oxford: Pergamon.

creatures. Yes, living species may be defined by their inability to mate and produce offspring with each other, and we may imagine that genera are categories of descendant species from some single ancient species, but biological nature is not itself structured as an ontology of mutually exclusive categories, and the so-called *chronospecies* show gradual variations in a single gene pool over large spans of time that illustrate the imperfection of the term *species*. One modern school of thought using the term *cladistics* proposes that speciation occurred very rapidly, and we should retain strict Linnaean taxonomy.[11] This prompted me to comment: "Thus the definition of species is inextricably tied up with competing conceptions of evolutionary process, and the nomenclature of a field is saturated with its major theoretical assumptions."[12]

Having *love* in mind as the example of expression, a remarkably apt social science example of linguistic ambiguity is a classic paper in development of computer translation, "A Four-letter Word in 'Lady Chatterley's Lover,'" by Angus McIntosh. In colloquial English, a *four-letter word* is an obscenity, which reminds us that language is constrained by social norms. As Wikipedia summarizes,

> Lady Chatterley's Lover is a novel by D. H. Lawrence, first published privately in 1928 in Italy, and in 1929 in France and Australia. An unexpurgated edition was not published openly in the United Kingdom until 1960, when it was the subject of a watershed obscenity trial against the publisher Penguin Books. Penguin won the case, and quickly sold 3 million copies. The book was also banned for obscenity in the United States, Canada, Australia, India and Japan. The book soon became notorious for its story of the physical (and emotional) relationship between a working class

[11] Cracraft, J. 1981. "Pattern and Process in Paleobiology: The Role of Cladistic Analysis in Systematic Paleontology." *Paleobiology* 7, no. 4, pp. 456–468; Ginerich, P.D. 1987. "Species in the Fossil Record: Concepts, Trends, and Transitions." *Paleobiology* 13, pp. 169–176.

[12] Bainbridge, W.S. 1994. "Scientific Nomenclature." In *The Encyclopedia of Language and Linguistics*, eds. R.E. Asher, 3685–3690, 3688. Oxford: Pergamon.

man and an upper class woman, its explicit descriptions of sex, and its use of then-unprintable words.[13]

McIntosh's essay concerns a multi-ironic four-letter verb, given that its first letter is not pronounced and it can be used as a synonym for *love*: *to know*.

Angus McIntosh was one of the inspirations for this book, since he was one of my uncles and played major professional roles in the convergence of humanities, social science, and computer science. In 1952, he founded what is now named The Angus McIntosh Centre for Historical Linguistics at the University of Edinburgh, which I visited in 1957 and 1965.[14] A prominent connection to the humanities is that he was a student and close friend of J.R.R. Tolkien and is given some credit for the invention of Hobbits.[15] During the Second World War, he decrypted German codes at the secret Ultra project at Bletchley Park, using hardware such as the mysterious Dragon device.[16] For a time in the 1960s he collaborated closely with Michael Halliday in development of theories of grammar that could explicitly be the basis for sophisticated machine translations of language.[17] His biggest computer-assisted project was the four huge volumes of *A Linguistic Atlas of Late Mediaeval English*.[18] A version named eLALME is available online today for anyone to use.[19]

McIntosh's essay used the verb *to know* in *Lady Chatterley's Lover* as an example of the difficulty of translating English literature into French, and to develop grammar-based methods that could be used in machine translations to resolve multiple meanings. Entering "know" into Google Translate today offers three definitions: "1. be aware of through observation,

---

[13]   en.wikipedia.org/wiki/Lady_Chatterley%27s_Lover

[14]   Giegerich, H. "Angus McIntosh, An Appreciation." www.amc.lel.ed.ac.uk/?page_id=238

[15]   tolkiengateway.net/wiki/Angus_McIntosh

[16]   Reeds, J. 2010. "American Dragon," *Cryptologia* 35, no. 1, pp. 22–41, 34.

[17]   McIntosh, A., and M.A.K. Haliday. 1966. *Patterns of Language: Papers in General, Descriptive and Applied Linguistics*. London: Longmans.

[18]   McIntosh, A., M.L. Samuels, and M. Benskin. 1986. *A Linguistic Atlas of Late Mediaeval English*. Aberdeen: Aberdeen University Press.

[19]   www.lel.ed.ac.uk/ihd/elalme/elalme_frames.html

inquiry, or information; 2. have developed a relationship with (someone) through meeting and spending time with them; be familiar or friendly with; 3. have sexual intercourse with (someone)." Suggested French equivalents of the first two are offered: "savoir (know, see, be aware, figure out, realize, sort out); connaître (know, experience, be acquainted, cognize, taste, ken)."[20] The last example for connaître, *ken*, links to the German word *kennen*, and to a significant extent English is considered a Germanic language. A Wikipedia article refers to "the nineteenth century song D'ye ken John Peel—'ken' meaning 'to be aware of' or 'to know' in some dialects of the North of England and Scotland."[21]

In translating between French and German, rather close correspondences exist: *savoir = wissen* and *connaître = kennen*. At the moment, Google Translate renders both French words into German as *wissen*, and both German words into French as *savoir*. However, a less artificial online dictionary agrees that the two languages share two distinct but sometimes overlapping concepts.[22] A common word like *savoir* or *wissen* may have multiple discernable meanings, but they chiefly refer to intellectual knowledge of a concept or set of facts. In contrast, *connaître* and *kennen* refer to the existence of a socioemotional relationship of personal familiarity. The fact that formal English has abandoned this distinction and uses *know* for both very different meanings obscures the challenge for computer scientists who are more comfortable with intellectual knowledge, who may therefore oversimplify their efforts to develop machine translation.

The main data in eLALME are structured rather like survey research, as the team of scholars went arduously through all the available Middle English writings dating from the years 1325 to 1450, marking on what they indeed called a *questionnaire* the instances of a careful selection of words and grammatical forms.[23] The exact spelling and presumably pronunciation of *know* varied, including: know, knowe, knaw, knawe, knauwe, and knauve. Today, *to know* is described as an irregular verb, and

[20] translate.google.com/#view=home&op=translate&sl=en&tl=fr&text=know

[21] en.wikipedia.org/wiki/John_Peel_(huntsman)

[22] en.pons.com/translate

[23] www.lel.ed.ac.uk/ihd/elalme/intros/atlas_gen_intro.html

a website explicitly for "dummies" reports: "verb = know, past = knew, past participle—known."[24] To the ear, heard as spoken words, these variants may have sounded very similar, but also indistinguishable from *no* without the grammatical and topic context of the sentence. Past participle forms in eLALME are: knowen, knawn, knawyn, knawen, knawne, and knawun.

Middle English ended when commerce and politics rendered London the center of authority for England, defining culture as well as other features of life. For centuries, the Académie Française has set formal standards for the French language.[25] In the 20th century both school textbooks and radio and TV news reporters set standards for English in the United States and other independent English-speaking nations. One might hypothesize that Internet-supported globalization will reduce the numbers of spoken languages to a dozen, with one official standard for each, rendering dialectology obsolete. Yet an equally plausible hypothesis is that in their daily communications people will combine aspects of multiple linguistic traditions in dynamic, idiosyncratic ways. Today, and for the foreseeable future, everyday conversation and literature flourish in many languages that belong to various families and possess idiosyncratic features that were the result of random historical events.

Communicating Emotion and Mystery

To be sure, many researchers on human–computer interaction have recognized the significance of human emotions.[26] However, machine translation of language really began and has been supported over the decades primarily by governments that sought to discover the practical rather than emotional secrets of competing governments, as at Bletchley Park, and this approach was facilitated by the fact that the opponent was well organized and used standardized if encrypted forms of communication. Thus, here we cannot assume that natural language processing is the solution

---

[24] www.dummies.com/education/language-arts/grammar/past-and-past-participles-of-common-irregular-english-verbs

[25] www.xn--acadmie-franaise-npb1a.fr

[26] Peter, C., and R. Beale., eds. 2008. *Affect and Emotion in HCI*. Berlin: Springer.

for all problems related to linguistic culture. Approaching languages as a medium for social relationships can be explored further by consideration of one of the most famous poems of all time, which Wikipedia provides in this form:

> Ille mi par esse deo videtur,
> ille, si fas est, superare divos,
> qui sedens adversus identidem te
> spectat et audit
> dulce ridentem, misero quod omnes
> eripit sensus mihi: nam simul te,
> Lesbia, aspexi, nihil est super mi
> <vocis in ore;>
> lingua sed torpet, tenuis sub artus
> flamma demanat, sonitu suopte
> tintinant aures, gemina teguntur
> lumina nocte.[27]

This is poem number 51, in the standard catalog for the Roman poet Gaius Valerius Catullus, who lived around the years 84 to 54 BC. Technically, that is one sentence, and early publications included no punctuation marks. Catullus Online offers an image of one early hand-written manuscript in which each line begins with the first letter in capitals but separated from the rest of its word, and the only punctuation is the period after *nocte*.[28] Many of the words are abbreviated; for example *esse* in the first line is written as two letters "e" with a line over them. Another old manuscript on the site avoids extreme abbreviations, but the oldest Catullus manuscript dates from the 9th century AD, and thus all are copies of copies of copies.[29] The line *vocis in ore* is a speculative reconstruction

---

[27] en.wikipedia.org/wiki/Catullus_51
[28] catullusonline.woodpecker.hu/uploads/O_13r_0032%7B48420_118%7D.jpg
[29] catullusonline.woodpecker.hu/uploads/G_12v_0029%7B48420_208%7D.jpg

of words that one copyist apparently missed. Entering this into Google Translate after removing the punctuation marks added by modern scholars gives an approximate and rather confused translation:

> That seems to be like a god
> if it is possible to surpass the gods, he
> He sits opposite you
> and hears
> all the sweet laughing again and again in my wretched state
> For once you senseless
> Lesbia looked nothing is left
> voice edge
> febrile fine
> flame ring
> My ears are covered
> lights at night

This automatic translation even omits words, beginning most obviously with *spectat*, because *spectat et audit* translates easily into English as "sees and hears," given that a *spectator* sees and one's *auditory* nerves hear. A complete translation might be: "sees you and hears... your sweet laughter." Here is the human translation Wikipedia quotes:

> He seems to me to be equal to a god,
> he, if it is permissible, seems to surpass the gods,
> who sitting opposite again and again
> watches and hears you
> sweetly laughing, which rips out all senses
> from miserable me: for at the same moment I look upon you,
> Lesbia, nothing is left for me
> <of my voice in my mouth;>
> But my tongue grows thick, a thin flame
> runs down beneath my limbs, with their own sound
> my ears ring, my twin lights (eyes)
> are covered by night.

Two key words in this poem are *mi* and *te*, *me* and *you*. Note that Latin distinguished the singular from the plural second person, while English uses *you* for both, having abandoned the singular *thou* long ago. This poem is like words spoken by Catullus in a conversation with Lesbia, or a letter written to her wishing he were *sedens adversus ... te*. When reciting this poem, one naturally adds tone, facial expressions, and hand gestures. It "feels" as if the best way to say *superare* is to stress and lengthen the third syllable, su-per-AHHHH-re, to look upward, and wave one's hand toward the heavens. Yes, *superare* can be translated "to surpass," but one of the sources at the classics-oriented digital library, The Perseus Project, translates *super* in terms of looking upward as "above, over, on top, thereupon, upon."[30] Given the flood of metaphors in this poem, who is Lesbia?

Her Wikipedia page says,

> Lesbia was the literary pseudonym used by the Roman poet Gaius Valerius Catullus (c. 82–52 BC) to refer to his lover. Lesbia is traditionally identified with Clodia, the wife of Quintus Caecilius Metellus Celer and sister of Publius Clodius Pulcher; her conduct and motives are maligned in Cicero's extant speech Pro Caelio, delivered in 56 BC.[31]

Why did Catullus not call her Clodia in the poem, given that her real name has the same metric cadence as Lesbia? Aside from the possibility he was then hiding their relations from the public, given her marriage to another man, the name Lesbia hints at the fact that this Latin poem is an adapted translation of a Greek poem by the Lesbian Sappho, who lived about 630 to 570. In one sense of the term, Sappho was definitely a Lesbian, because she was from the island named Lesbos. Scholars have long debated the details of her real life, but many deduced from some of her surviving poetry that she indeed was a female homosexual, and that is how the term *lesbian* got its meaning in the English language. The many cultural subdivisions of ancient Greek culture explored a variety of gender

---

[30] www.perseus.tufts.edu/hopper/text?doc=Perseus%3Atext%3A1999.04.0059%3Aentry%3Dsuper2

[31] en.wikipedia.org/wiki/Lesbia

relations, and there may not have been a rigorous classification scheme describing erotic preferences or sexual behavior.[32] So any computer or even person that can translate poetry with perfect accuracy from one language and culture to another ... *ille mi par esse deo videtur.*

For two centuries, humanists and social scientists have attempted to develop logical classification systems for cultural variations. Among the most influential was the Apollonian–Dionysian dichotomy proposed by Friedrich Nietzsche in German in 1872: *Die Geburt der Tragödie aus dem Geiste der Musik*, usually translated into English as *The Birth of Tragedy from the Spirit of Music.*[33] Named after the comparable but competing Greek gods, Apollo and Dionysus, these two archetypes represent opposite modes of response to human existence. The Apollonian is cool, rational, and today we would place computer science in this category. The Dionysian is hot, lustful, romantic, and expresses itself through music and dance. From Arthur Schopenhauer's 1818 book, *The World as Will and Idea*, Nietzsche also took the idea that Apollonianism was the *principium individuationis*—the principle of individuation—which marked solitary philosophers who sought to understand the world through private contemplation or the exercise of their individual intellects.[34] In contrast, Dionysianism is a form of extreme collective intoxication experienced in emotional group rituals and drunken festivals.

When Ruth Benedict applied Nietzsche's concepts to anthropology in her 1934 book *Patterns of Culture*, she suggested Dionysians could be individualistic. Indeed, a deep reading of *The Birth of Tragedy* suggests that Nietzsche was struggling to distinguish two potentially orthogonal dichotomies: cold versus hot and individual versus collective. He actually mentioned a third category, the Buddhist, that deemphasizes both self and society. Logically, there must be a fourth type, which emphasizes both. In writing his most famous work, *Also Sprach Zatharathustra*, Nietzsche may have been on a quest for a cultural convergence of cool, hot, individual, and cultural. Can Google Translate handle its most quoted text?

---

[32] en.wikipedia.org/wiki/Sappho

[33] Bainbridge, W.S. 2010. "Burglarizing Nietzsche's Tomb." *Journal of Evolution and Technology* 21, no. 1, 37–54; jetpress.org/v21/bainbridge.htm

[34] Schopenhauer, A. 1883–1886. *The World as Will and Idea*. London: Trübner.

Oh Mensch! Gieb Acht!
Was spricht die tiefe Mitternacht?
"Ich schlief, ich schlief -,
Aus tiefem Traum bin ich erwacht:-
Die Welt ist tief,
Und tiefer als der Tag gedacht.
Tief ist ihr Weh -,
Lust—tiefer noch als Herzeleid:
Weh spricht: Vergeh!
Doch alle Lust will Ewigkeit -,
- will tiefe, tiefe Ewigkeit!"

Oh man! Eight!
What does the deep midnight say?
"I slept, I slept -,
From a deep dream I woke up: -
The world is deep,
And thought deeper than the day.
Deep is her woes -,
Lust—even deeper than heartache:
Woe say, Pardon!
But all lust wants eternity -,
- wants deep, deep eternity!"

While not hopeless, the Google Translate version makes definite mistakes and cannot divine the deep meaning of this stanza. By translating *Mensch* as *man*, the NLP system backs into the gender problems in languages. An online dictionary says that *Mensch* means "person" or "human," not exactly "man."[35] It can mean "mankind," and until recently "man" was often used in this sense. Yes, *der Mensch* is a masculine noun in German, but grammatically masculine, not biologically. In the Catullus verse, *sensus* is masculine, in the fourth declension category, not the more common

---

[35] www.collinsdictionary.com/dictionary/german-english/mensch

second declension illustrated by the word *servus* meaning slave, not a concept dear to the heart of Catullus. Yet *sensus* is an abstract concept related to the English word "sense," and thus lacking biological gender.

Translating *Gieb Acht!* as "Eight!" is the worst mistake, rather a good metaphor for the numerical obsessions of computer scientists. *Acht* does not refer to the number eight but to "attention," as in the stereotypical military command, *Achtung. Gieb* is an imperative form of *geben*, "to give." Gieb Acht! can mean "pay attention" or "take care," but the literary translation is "take heed!" The connotations of later words are also distorted by the automatic translation. For example, German nouns are capitalized, so *Lust* simplistically becomes *lust*, yet all five standard translations by scholars into English render it as *joy*, even while they disagree about *Herzeleid*, rendering it either as *grief, woe, misery*, or two of them as *agony*.[36]

It may seem unfair to use Google Translate as the representative for natural language processing, because better systems would concentrate upon a body of text representing a specific subculture of interest, such as a technical field, and adjust its dictionary to improve translation of new documents within the same corpus. Yet both fancy literature and ordinary talk are flexible in focus and vocabulary. In *Also Sprach Zatharathustra*, "acht" appears hundreds of times, but almost always as a syllable of a longer word, and only six times as exactly this word, twice in the poem which is repeated, twice in elaborations on the poem, and twice in similar contexts. It is easy for anyone to check this, because the German text is available at Gutenberg.org, although the Google Chrome browser search engine counts *ächt*, which Google Translate wisely renders as *genuine* or *real*, as if it were *acht*.[37] A sentence that Google Translate handles well suggests the challenge: "Was ist es, das Achten und Verachten und Werth und Willen schuf? (What is it, the respect and contempt and value and will created?)." Like Latin, German employs many forms of the same noun or verb. English has few grammatical forms but a huge vocabulary, often adapting a Latin word as it did for *respect*, while German tends to reassemble words and fragments from its own culture.

---

[36] en.wikipedia.org/wiki/Zarathustra%27s_roundelay

[37] www.gutenberg.org/cache/epub/7205/pg7205.txt

The title of Nietzsche's masterwork, *Also Sprach Zarathustra*, has been translated alternately *Thus Spoke Zarathustra*, or intentionally anachronistically as *Thus Spake Zarathustra*. However, "Zarathustra" is often rendered as *Zoroaster*, the name of a "spiritual leader and ethical philosopher who taught a spiritual philosophy of self-realization and realization of the Divine."[38] We may well wonder how much Nietzsche was influenced by Zoroastrian thinking. The best translation of the meaning of the *Oh Mensch* song for English speakers in not in English or ancient Persian, but in music, the 1896 orchestral tone poem by Richard Strauss.[39] It took on new meaning when used as the theme music for the epic 1968 movie, *2001: A Space Odyssey*.[40]

Similarly, the poem by Catullus was set to music by Carl Orff in his 1943 cantata, *Catulli Carmina*, that tells the story of the stormy relationship between Catullus and Clodia, beginning ideally and ending disastrously.[41] It is dramatically framed by a different Catullus fragment: "*Odi et amo. Quare id faciam fortasse requiris. Nescio, sed fieri sentio et excrucior.* (I hate and I love. Why I do this, perhaps you ask. I know not, but I feel it happening and I am tortured.)."[42] Note that *excrucior* is related to the English word "excruciating." In the first person singular, *sentio* means "I sense," from the verb for "to discern by sense, feel, hear, see, perceive, be sensible of something."[43] *Nescio* means "I don't know" and is a standard verb that does not quite exist as such in English, with the meaning of being unknowing, ignorant, or unaware.[44] The root, *scio*, means *I know*, understand, perceive, have knowledge of, or am skilled in, and is the origin of our word *science*.[45] We certainly will not mention the Latin student joke about conjugation of this verb: *scio, slippere, falli, bumptum*.[46] (To

---

[38] en.wikipedia.org/wiki/Zoroaster

[39] en.wikipedia.org/wiki/Also_sprach_Zarathustra_(Strauss)

[40] en.wikipedia.org/wiki/2001:_A_Space_Odyssey_(film)

[41] en.wikipedia.org/wiki/Catulli_Carmina

[42] en.wikipedia.org/wiki/Catullus_85

[43] www.perseus.tufts.edu/hopper/text?doc=Perseus%3Atext%3A1999.04.0060%3Aentry%3Dsentio

[44] www.perseus.tufts.edu/hopper/morph?l=Nescio&la=la

[45] www.perseus.tufts.edu/hopper/morph?l=scio&la=la

[46] Bainbridge, W.S. 2015. *The Meaning and Value of Spaceflight*, 117. Springer.

decode, read *scio* as *ski-o*.) Yes? But, the Latin language did not actually have a word for *yes*, and its word *sic* that became *si* in subsequent Romance languages for *yes* originally meant *thus*.

During the year 2018, the English-language Wikipedia page for Catullus received 116,953 views, which was completely eclipsed by the 2,148,557 views of Nietzsche's page. Given our focus here on translation, we should consider the fact that there are many Wikipedias, in different languages, including both Latin and German, although unfortunately neither of those incorporate the pageviews statistical function. Table 6.1 reports the pageviews for the five artists across nine Wikipedias, arranged in descending order of Catullus pageviews. As of April 2019, the English-language version of Wikipedia offered 5,844,000 articles, nearly 4 times the 1,522,000 articles in the Italian version. Yet Catullus earned nearly as many Italian pageviews as English ones, presumably because he belongs to the heritage of the people of Italy. The last two columns of the table express ratios of pageviews for pairs of authors, and in the Italian version Catullus garnered 109.3 percent of the pageviews of Sappho, but in the Greek version only 6.7 percent.

Google Translate was actually very helpful in collecting these data, and I often asked Google's Chrome browser to translate a page into English. Finding pages about specific people is relatively easy across languages, because a page typically has near the beginning the name of the person in that person's native language, such as Σαπφώ for Sappho, and the identity can be confirmed by a portrait or birthdate. But sometimes key words were necessary, and for some languages it helped when looking for the pageview statistics or, for example, confirming that the Japanese version like the German one lacked them. The crucial lesson is that advanced information technology tools can be very helpful when doing research in the humanities, but the main work must be done by a human scholar.

A Commercial and Cultural Success Story

A Polish videogame named *Witcher 3: Wild Hunt* was analyzed in my 2016 book, *Virtual Sociocultural Convergence*, in a chapter about what

Table 6.1 Wikipedia pageviews of five creators across languages

Language	Gaius Catullus	Sappho (Σαπφώ)	Friedrich Nietzsche	Richard Strauss	Carl Orff	Catullus/ Sappho	Catullus/ Nietzsche
English	116,953	473,240	2,148,557	312,483	157,137	24.7%	5.4%
Italian	110,275	100,877	326,670	62,187	26,270	109.3%	33.8%
Spanish	41,954	147,082	1,024,171	65,570	53,492	28.5%	4.1%
Russian	27,619	65,743	436,088	37,617	40,272	42.0%	6.3%
French	22,415	59,660	348,752	52,831	54,360	37.6%	6.4%
Portuguese	4,760	26,536	459,981	13,715	16,682	17.9%	1.0%
Polish	3,933	32,225	161,353	14,751	13,382	12.2%	2.4%
Chinese	2,384	7,703	140,917	17,388	24,333	30.9%	1.7%
Greek	1,468	22,024	43,652	3,123	3,344	6.7%	3.4%

I call the Silicon Law, the fact that computer technology can enhance human freedom in some ways, even as it dominates us in other ways:

> In order to see a wide range of autonomy issues in computer games that stimulate reality, it was necessary to start with an example of high quality that imposes strict controls on the player, while technically permitting increased autonomy at some cost. The ideal example was *Witcher 3: Wild Hunt*, a highly acclaimed and popular 2015 game with great psychological and cultural depth. The player is like an actor assigned a highly scripted role, with limited options on how to play it.[47]

For much of the 20th century, Poland was overshadowed and often dominated by Germany and Russia, but again Poland has become significant in world culture, as hinted at by the fact that the global home page for Wikipedia includes Polish among the 10 featured languages, all of which have over a million pages.

The Witcher series is based on literature by Andrzej Sapkowski, and his page in the Polish version of Wikipedia received 680,647 pageviews in the period from July 1, 2015, through May 3, 2019. His page in the English language version got 887,888. Here we can dispense with pageviews as the unit of analysis and note that the page was initially created on August 19, 2002, by someone using the name Akir whose profile says he lives in the Polish city of Bialystok. The page for Andrzej Sapkowski in the English version of Wikipedia is a few months older, having been created on December 10, 2001, by someone using the name Szopen who at that time reported being a student at Poznań University of Technology in Poland. Vast data about the social structure of Wikipedia topics can be gleaned from the "view history" tab on each page; for example, the Polish and English versions of Sapkowski's page had 66 and 78 editors, respectively, and that indeed is the route to find the pageviews. Here our focus is language, and it is interesting to note that within a year after the January 15, 2001 launch of the English language version of Wikipedia, a

---

[47] Bainbridge, W.S. 2016. *Virtual Sociocultural Convergence: Human Sciences of Computer Games*, 97. London: Springer.

Polish student had posted an article about Andrzej Sapkowski on it, and the Polish version of Wikipedia also launched in that year, on September 26, 2001. As the English page for *The Witcher* proclaims, it is an excellent example of how popular media can be both international and multimedia:

> The books have been adapted into a film, a television series, video games, and a graphic novel series. The series of novels is known as the *Witcher Saga*. The short stories and novels have been translated into numerous languages, including English ... The books have been described as having a cult following in Poland, the Czech Republic, Hungary, Slovakia, Ukraine, Romania, Russia, Serbia, Bulgaria and other Central and Eastern European countries. The video games have been very successful, and as of March 2018, they have sold over 33 million copies worldwide.[48]

The fact that the Wikipedias preserve the histories of their pages allows scholars and social scientists to chart the development of recent popular cultures. Also, machine translation can be a valuable tool, even though the results are flawed. It was a simple matter, while using the Chrome browser, to request English translations of the Polish pages, and also copy words and passages into Google Translate run on a separate page. Here is the beginning of the original 2001 English Wikipedia article about Sapkowski, followed by automatic translations of the beginnings of both the original and current Polish pages. We can see that the original pages were written independently, rather than one being the translation of the other, and that the biography has evolved over the years:

> Original English: "'Andrzej Sapkowski'", born 1948, Polish [[Fantasy|fantasy]] writer. His first novel, [[Hexer]], was published in [[Fantastyka]] in 1986 and was enormous success. "Hexer" cycle consists of few novels and books ("Wiedzmin" 1990, "Miecz przeznaczenia" 1992, "Ostatnie zyczenie" 1993, "Krew Elfow" 1994, "Czas pogardy" 1995, "Chrzest ognia" 1996, "Wieza

---

[48] en.wikipedia.org/wiki/The_Witcher

jaskolki" 1997, "Pani jeziora" 1999) which made him bestselling author in [[Poland]] in 1990s.

Original Polish: "Andrzej Sapkowski" (born 1948) Polish writer [[fantasy]], Economic education. Married. He began his literary career as a translator. He gained popularity through the cycle of short stories and a five-volume novel about [Witcher | The Witcher]]. (the first story appeared in December 1986 in the monthly 'Fantasy'). In addition, he published an essay on the Knights of the Round Table "The World of King Arthur. Maladie", lexicon of a fantasy lover "Manuscript found in Dragon Cave", Guide for people starting playing [[RPG]] pt. "Eye of Yrrhedes" and many stories and articles in magazines and collections of short stories.

Current Polish: Andrzej Sapkowski (born on June 21, 1948 in Łódź)—a Polish fantasy writer, an economist by profession [1]. Creator of the Witcher character. It is most often after Lemie, translated by the Polish author of fantasy. In 2012, the Minister of Culture and National Heritage, Bogdan Zdrojewski, awarded him with the silver medal Gloria Artis [3].

Uncertainties in the results of machine translation can be explored by humans, which is easiest when they are as obvious as this perplexing sentence: "It is most often after Lemie, translated by the Polish author of fantasy." The identity of "Lemie" is easy to determine, because the name links to the Polish Wikipedia page for Stanisław Lem.[49] So a better translation would be "He is the most often translated Polish author of fantasy after Stanisław Lem." Table 6.2 compares the creation dates and pageviews for a subset of Wikipedia pages about *The Witcher* "franchise" or "mythos."

Geralt of Rivia is the main protagonist in the stories, and his English page began as a "stub from pl wiki." Similarly, the original English page for the TV series "The Hexer" is noted "from pl wiki." So material in

---

[49] pl.wikipedia.org/wiki/Stanis%C5%82aw_Lem

Table 6.2 Comparison of a cultural Franchise in two versions of Wikipedia

Name	Category	English Wikipedia		Polish Wikipedia	
		Creation Date	Pageviews	Creation Date	Pageviews
The Witcher	Franchise	December 10, 2001	4,080,258	April 30, 2002	184,676
Andrzej Sapkowski	Author	December 10, 2001	887,888	August 19, 2002	680,647
Geralt of Rivia	Character	November 16, 2007	925,193	November 11, 2004	273,997
The Last Wish	Book	September 6, 2007	666,223	July 29, 2006	157,243
Sword of Destiny	Book	October 1, 2013	339,076	July 29, 2006	107,377
The Hexer	Movie	May 12, 2006	27,315	February 16, 2006	126,923
The Hexer	TV series	March 1, 2009	247,930	August 19, 2008	100,740
The Witcher	Videogame	September 4, 2006	2,844,004	November 5, 2006	286,789
The Witcher 2: Assassins of Kings	Videogame	September 18, 2009	1,501,541	September 19, 2009	132,303
The Witcher 3: Wild Hunt	Videogame	February 6, 2013	5,163,313	February 6, 2013	373,221
CD Projekt	Game company	February 9, 2004	1,131,290	January 24, 2006	63,622

different-language wikis may either be produced independently or translated across. Both pages for the movie note it was a spin-off from the TV series, and of course they, like the videogames (produced by CD Projekt, a Polish company), were spin-offs from the literature. While originating within the Polish language and culture, *The Witcher* productions were aimed at an international audience and are an excellent example of cross-cultural creativity that scholars may benefit from studying. The English article noted the rich traditions involved even just in the translation of the title:

> Sapkowski chose *wiedźmin* as the male equivalent of the Polish word for witch (*wiedźma*). In his book 2005 book-interview *Historia i Fantastyka Sapkowski* noted that the word "witcher" is a natural male version of the English word "witch", and implied that the similarity between those two words, as well as between the German terms, was the inspiration coining *wiedźmin* as a new Polish word. Polish video game designer Adrian Chmielarz claimed to have invented the translation of *wiedźmin* into English as *witcher* around 1996–1997. Although *wiedźmin* is now usually translated into English as "witcher", an earlier translation of the title was "hexer" (the title of the 2001 film adaptation and the first official English translation in the 2000 short story collection *Chosen by Fate: Zajdel Award Winner Anthology*); *Hexe* and *Hexer* are the German words for "witch" and "warlock" respectively. CD Projekt used "witcher" for the title of its 2007 English release of the video game, and Danusia Stok used it in her translation of *Ostanie życzenie* that was published the same year. Michael Kandel however used "spellmaker" in his 2010 translation of "Wiedźmin" short story for *A Book of Polish Monsters* anthology.[50]

Rather than expand this analysis to other languages through Wikipedia, and adding a few other related pages, we should recognize that Fandom.com, earlier named Wikia, supports Witcher-related wikis in 22

---

[50] en.wikipedia.org/wiki/The_Witcher

languages offering a total of 41,781 articles, as listed in Table 6.3. Using similar technology to that of Wikipedia, but organizationally unrelated, as reported by Wikipedia:

> the most common interest of its users is in popular fiction franchises of films, games, books, and other media, due to the considerable limitation of such detailed information by Wikipedia's notability policies. This contributed to the service being renamed to Fandom. The main purpose of articles in a Wikia community is to cover information and discussion on a particular topic in a

Table 6.3 The same subculture in wikis of different languages

Language	Title	Pages	Rank	WAM
English	Witcher	10,388	46	98.51
Russian	Ведьмака	6,565	309	91.06
Polish	Wied min	6,893	534	85.47
Spanish	Brujo	1,168	2,599	43.56
Portuguese	Witcher	1,377	2,646	42.49
German	Hexer	4,492	2,741	40.18
Italian	Witcher	3,152	3,187	31.26
French	Sorceleur	3,091	3,921	16.75
Czech	Zaklína e	1,742		
Ukranian	Відьмак	1,109		
Arabic	الويتشر	601		
Hungarian	Witcher	444		
Lithuanian	Raganius	200		
Greek	Witcher	122		
Vietnamese	Witcher	99		
Slovak	Zaklína	89		
Dutch	Witcher	65		
Chinese	Witcher	51		
Swedish	Häxkarl	43		
Serbian	Witcher	40		
Finnish	Noituri	37		
Danish	Witcher	13		

much greater and more comprehensive detail level than what can be found on Wikipedia articles.[51]

Although each wiki is a separate encyclopedia, there is a central search tool which can be told to search any combination of language and medium and that also has a popularity measure called Wiki Activity Monitor:

> The WAM is calculated daily for the top 5,000 wiki sites and includes an overall rank, a vertical rank, and a score from 0 to 100. The WAM rankings are sensitive to real-world events and change frequently, capturing the latest trends from FANDOM's wikis.[52]

The algorithm for calculating the WAM is kept secret, to discourage manipulation of the data on which it is based, and the vertical rank is calculated in terms of the particular medium such as games or books.

We see that the English language Witcher wiki had a very high WAM, 98.51 out of 100, and earned an overall rank of 46 out of 5,000 wikis on April 26, 2019. Speaking of translation challenges, we should note that a very popular wiki earns a high WAM number, but a low rank. As with Wikipedia pageviews, this database can be used to measure sudden changes in popularity of a cultural product, for example, triggered by some special event, such as the release of a new game or the final episode of a TV series. Table 6.4 surveys the numbers of pages across the six media in Fandom.com's classification system, across the six non-English languages that had more than 50 wikis on whatever range of topics. The seventh category, *lifestyle*, is excluded from the analysis of the comprehensive measures, because it is residual rather than meaningful. The huge number of Russian lifestyle pages reflects the fact that it contains a 204,734-page Virtual KLab "где каждый может присоединится к коллективным научным изысканиям и популяризации науки" ("where everyone can join the collective scientific research and popularization of science").[53]

---

[51] en.wikipedia.org/wiki/Wikia

[52] community.fandom.com/wiki/WAM

[53] vlab.wikia.org/ru/

Table 6.4 Statistics of popular media in non-English Wikis

Wiki categories	Spanish	Russian	German	French	Polish	Portuguese
Wiki pages:						
TV	188,656	63,086	91,152	38,415	55,623	38,915
Games	259,779	262,824	193,030	117,578	130,799	65,050
Books	38,389	20,926	30,931	18,877	16,809	6,008
Comics	67,906	47,760	18,776	47,654	22,294	26,982
Music	20,381	1,908	1,571	61,645	0	0
Movies	44,480	46,993	42,842	28,054	24,502	20,738
Total	619,591	443,497	378,302	312,223	250,027	157,693
Comprehensive measures:						
Wikis	246	339	119	123	107	70
Pages per wiki	2,519	1,308	3,179	2,538	2,337	2,253
Mean WAM	43.69	47.50	42.93	46.79	45.63	37.84
Correlation WAM-pages	0.44	0.39	0.41	0.18	0.31	0.37
Excluded from analysis:						
Lifestyle	78,570	262,859	36,439	11,371	15,261	2,414

A vast number of cultural science studies can be conducted using data from these wikis, although scholars would want to coordinate with other data and exercise a certain caution. We do not know which of the pages were posted by actual fans of a particular franchise or mythos, versus employees of the corporation that profits from its popularity. This is also true for Wikipedia. Some of the research challenges illustrate the complex nature of worldwide online culture. For example, Fandom.com has only 20 wikis in the Japanese language, two of them about *Star Wars* and one each about *Thomas the Tank Engine, Star Trek, Marvel, The Walking Dead, Harry Potter, Game of Thrones,* and these non-Japanese games: *Elder Scrolls, Halo,* and *No Mans Sky.* Yet many of the wikis in the TV, games, and comics categories of the other languages concern products of the Japanese anime and manga tradition.

Conclusion

A vast number and diversity of information technology tools will be of value to students and researchers of cultural science. Which of them should be termed *artificial intelligence* is open to debate, but I suggest that any outcome of that debate would be useless. The main functions and biases of each tool must be understood by users, and each will have a certain range of applications that deserves its own term. I use the term *artificial social intelligence* to refer to systems that employ computer or comparable information technologies and that function intelligently through the convergence of multiple trains of thought. How the intelligence is distributed between the machine and the user is a detail of each tool and application. In the context of cultural science, which itself has a broad definition, the intelligence must be social, because the data under study was produced by one or more members of a particular culture and subculture—a German philosopher in the case of Nietzsche—and the user probably intends the result to be socially relevant, for example, helping philosophy classes at a college understand Nietzsche or be properly mystified by his writings. Of course, there is ample room to debate whether some form of future general artificial intelligence can ever replace humanistic scholars in the study of literature. My own position is that this technical revolution could not happen unless machines led the same kinds of lives as humans, something that should be prevented even if it proves possible.

CHAPTER 7

Challenges and Responses for Public Policy and Investment

Convergence of artificial intelligence with the humanities and social sciences can help AI deal with major criticisms, both by humanizing it and by improving its social consequences. Every powerful technology can be used to cause harm, if it is in the hands of careless or evil people. A deep but largely unrecognized truth that I have been exploring in other publications is that many areas of science and technology have stalled and are achieving less progress than in the past, if any progress at all.[1] Some journalists have noted this desperate situation, but most scientists and engineers seem to deny the truth, many of them flocking to artificial intelligence because it is currently claiming the potential for revolutionary progress. Over two decades ago, John Horgan documented "the end of science," at least in the sciences closest to physics.[2] At times, the judgment of journalists becomes rather harsh, yet plausibly correct, as in "A Waste of 1,000 Research Papers" written by Ed Young for *The Atlantic*, who summarized the failure of research to identify significant genetic causes of depression, thus rendering diagnosis and treatment more problematic

---

[1] Bainbridge, W.S. 1997. "The Omicron Point: Sociological Application of the Anthropic Theory." In *Chaos and Complexity in Sociology: Myths, Models and Theory*, eds. R.A. Eve, S. Horsfall, and M.E. Lee, 91–101. Thousand Oaks, California: Sage Publications; Bainbridge, W.S. 2017. *Dynamic Secularization*. Cham, Switzerland: Springer.

[2] Horgan, J. 1996. *The End of Science*. Reading, MA: Addison-Wesley.

than we had hoped, a cause of depression if ever there was one.[3] Over half a century ago I attended a lecture at Yale by a prominent nuclear physicist who predicted development within five years of practical nuclear fusion power, giving us endless energy with very little pollution. He was wrong by literally more than an order of magnitude, because we aren't even close today. And I cannot forget the memory from December 1972, as I stood by night on a Florida beach and watched the launch of the last human voyage to the moon. That year also marked the end of the U.S. program to develop nuclear-powered rockets, which may explain why colonization of the planet Mars has not begun.

Facebook Groups Concerning Artificial Intelligence

A plausible environment for public debate about the human consequences of artificial intelligence is the popular social medium Facebook, because it contains many groups that are oriented to technology and discussion of diverse issues. Essentially all forms of social media have some of the qualities of recommender systems, obviously so in the case of Facebook. Extensive studies by many researchers have examined many dimensions of this extremely popular medium, as it evolved from the online expression of the social networks of college students into a major platform for advertising. While Facebook serves many social functions, several can be described as forms of advertising, from the use of one's personal profile to promote one's career, to the extensive creation of groups that serve as propaganda broadcasters for social movements and professions.

In a recent book, *The Social Structure of Online Communities*, I explored how Facebook groups are linked by people who belong to two or more having the same general topic, the diversity of examples covering the TV series *Westworld*, the National Space Society and Transhumanist social movements, the town of Greenwich in Connecticut, the Process Church of The Final Judgment, open source computer programming professional groups in India, and support groups for the imprisoned whistleblower

---

[3] Yong, E.D. 2019. "A Waste of 1,000 Research Papers: Decades of Early Research on the Genetics of Depression were Built on Nonexistent Foundations. How did that Happen?" *The Atlantic*, May 17, 2019, www.theatlantic.com/science/archive/2019/05/waste-1000-studies/589684

with the iconic name Reality Winner.[4] For *Family History Digital Libraries* I tried a more experiential or experimental method, creating a secret Facebook group named Bailiwick Archives, to which two dozen members of my family belong and where we privately share pictures, documents, and memories of our shared heritage.[5] For this current project, at the end of 2018 I created a closed Facebook group, Artificial Intelligence Meditations (AIM), with the motto "Take AIM!" It served as a news hub related to artificial intelligence controversies, serving a small network of somewhat like-minded scholars and critics of AI.

There are three primary categories of Facebook groups that differ in terms of privacy with respect to the general public, although the Facebook company has access to all the information. At the end of January 2019, to provide new information sources for AIM, I used the regular Facebook search tool to find groups explicitly focused on artificial intelligence, discovering 31 with at least 2,000 members each, to which I requested membership. Some automatically administered a few questions to each applicant, and any of their administrators could have checked my personal profile or sent me a message, but I received no further questions and was quickly admitted to 29 of the groups. After six weeks, two of the public groups had not acted on my membership request, which suggests they were primarily advertising tools for their administrators. Table 7.1 offers information about the 29 I joined, relevant to understanding a few of the more obvious features of the recommendation system.

During the somewhat complex process of joining these 29 groups, I noted any information that Facebook provided to guide my decisions. When a closed group actively invites people to join, they can temporarily see the postings and form the same kind of judgment always available for public groups. The results of a group search give the approximate membership size for both public and closed groups and often also report a statistic on the number of recent posts that suggests how active versus inactive the group is. The numbers of members and administrators given

---

[4] Bainbridge, W.S. 2020. *The Social Structure of Online Communities.* Cambridge, England: Cambridge University Press.
[5] Bainbridge, W.S. 2018. *Family History Digital Libraries.* Cham, Switzerland: Springer.

Table 7.1 Membership statistics for artificial intelligence Facebook groups

Group topic areas (not the group names)	Type	Members	Admins	Harvard	Friends
Artificial intelligence (AI), neural networks, deep learning	Public	195,338	5	704	158
Data mining, machine learning (ML), HCI	Public	89,351	14	205	109
The real-world happenings of AI	Public	50,247	5	152	80
Creation of super-intelligent machines	Closed	43,569	18	165	302
ML, data analytics, and AI	Public	39,766	4	87	49
Humor: no learning too deep, no meme too spicy	Public	36,579	6	153	41
Deep learning, the latest explosion in AI	Public	23,170	2	88	65
AI and ML	Closed	18,348	2	53	11
AI, DL, ML, and more	Closed	17,968	4	65	28
Impossible futuristic extraordinary new software AI	Closed	16,283	2	46	27
ML, AI, and robotics	Public	14,898	1	36	9
AI without taking advantage of any living organism	Public	13,325	4	54	10
DL, ML, Data Science, Blockchain, and AI	Public	9,684	1	26	18
For extraordinary software programmers and thinkers	Public	9,377	5	17	33
Discussions on research papers in AI	Public	9,045	2	25	19
Latest advances... to commercialize ideas in the end	Public	8,636	2	42	26
New innovations in AI and ML	Public	8,224	6	30	43

Group topic areas (not the group names)	Type	Members	Admins	Harvard	Friends
AI–ML subgroup of Hackathon Hackers	Public	8,068	2	57	16
Sharing humor and philosophy about AI	Closed	7,428	4	22	0
Info on Big Data, Data Science, and ML careers	Closed	6,887	3	16	4
Evolutionary algorithms such as genetic programming	Closed	5,840	1	28	59
AI in health care	Public	5,265	10	36	101
The future of AI	Public	4,840	3	48	172
Deploying of aggregated artificial intelligent solutions	Public	3,962	7	45	385
Sharing AI–DL articles, videos, and podcasts	Public	2,782	4	11	9
Applied AI for sales, marketing, customer experience	Closed	2,726	6	60	61
Our shared reality is a computer simulation, or will be	Public	2,713	12	21	94
AI and ML for product and startup people	Closed	2,684	3	21	7
Robots, chatbots, messaging and AI	Closed	2,414	3	21	52

in Table 7.1 came from the membership list after I had joined each group. The "Harvard" and "Friends" columns report data Facebook offered before I had joined any of the groups. When I set up my personal profile, I included the information "studied sociology at Harvard University," and Facebook would automatically tell me how many other members of a group had also listed a connection to Harvard. This kind of connection could be a rough measure of one's culture of origin, but not really relevant to my own searches for groups, because I am doing research studies on a sequence of different topics, rather than socializing with friends or family or even colleagues.

Group size is a measure of popularity, of course, but may not often be a good measure of the cultural location of the group. When I asked Excel to tell me the correlation between the number of members and number of Harvard people across these 29 groups, it reported 0.98, a number closer to 1.00 than we would expect to see in empirical data. The correlation between a group's size and the number of my Facebook "friends" who belong to it is much lower, only 0.25, and the largest number of friends are in the group that is ranked number 24, with just 3,962 members, compared with the largest group which has 195,338. We cannot be sure of the extent to which the number of Harvard people in a group represent the equivalent of a random sample of people interested more generally in groups that have intellectual topics. My list of "friends" totaled 3,030 at the time the data were collected, but most of those were people I had befriended, or who had befriended me, in the process of my earlier Facebook research studies. Thus the exact meaning of Facebook measures like these is uncertain, and other kinds of data may be necessary to resolve such issues.

Nearly all of the 29 groups are information and encouragement activities for mostly young people who seek career advancement in computer and information technology occupations. Their posts tend to be copies of news items, and on any given day several groups would have the same news, even the same links to the original sources. Two of the groups were humor-oriented, but sharing almost exclusively "in jokes" for the same IT career community, often posting the Facebook equivalent of cartoons. A couple of groups were looking toward a more distant and speculative future, including Artificial General Intelligence and the theory that our "real" world is actually a very advanced computer simulation. But even these groups serve about the same population of career-promoters, albeit on the margins of their community. I found very few news items or discussions that were fundamentally critical of artificial intelligence, and the mood was effusively optimistic about AI. To find criticisms of AI, I mainly had to look in technology journalism aimed at a wider but educated public, and in discussions within non-profit organizations.

Eight Targets of AIM

Many scientists, engineers, and governments are promoting what they call *artificial intelligence*, without a thorough critique of the validity of their concepts or evaluation of possible harm that could result from implementing them. In 2018, both the Association for Computing Machinery and the Institute of Electrical and Electronics Engineers conducted major re-examinations of their professional ethics standards, and indeed morality is a major component of culture in general.[6] However, there is little reason to believe that professional ethics have much power in today's conflicted world. At the same time, the continuing financial crisis in journalism, largely created by free online access to news, is pushing journalists to write stories that are ever more emotional, possibly even in technology areas. At least since the 1920s when the drama *R.U.R.* and the movie *Metropolis* dramatized the potential danger of artificial intelligence, the public sphere has been flooded with irrational horror fantasies that people may take too seriously.

The purpose of this section is to note eight different possible mechanisms by which artificial intelligence could cause harm and to consider briefly how rendering AI social could turn the balance toward benefit. When Artificial Intelligence Meditations launched, these eight were in its self-description as a communication hub where thoughtful people shared information that provides insights into issues like these. Over the first 6 months of 2019, about 200 online reports, some from organizations and some from journalists, were linked to the group page, greatly enhancing the background for the following analysis.

1. Pro-AI rhetoric contains many exaggerations, for example, calling machine learning an advanced form of artificial intelligence, when it really is just an ornate addition to classical multivariate statistical methods, such as factor analysis that is nearly a century old.

---

[6] www.acm.org/articles/bulletins/2018/july/new-code-of-ethics-released; standards.ieee.org/news/2018/ieee-launches-ecpais.html

This book has already suggested two problems the author believes are objective criticisms of AI: (1) AI rhetoric lumps together many kinds of algorithm, while ignoring their heritage in social statistics, and (2) given that human intelligence is social, for many humanly valuable applications the algorithms themselves must also be social, and thus embedded in or embodying specific human cultures. But there is a different criticism lurking slightly in the background of public misgivings about AI: religious definitions of human thought and perception.

A cultural factor seldom mentioned in government support for AI is religion, although one of the classic assertions of sociology, in the works of pioneers like Max Weber and Robert K. Merton, was that science was far more compatible with Protestantism than with Catholicism.[7] Robotics expert Masahiro Mori has cogently argued that artificial intelligence is especially compatible with Buddhism.[8] Conceivably, the religion factor partly explains why east Asian nations have been far more active in developing AI and computer technologies more generally than Latin American nations. Moderate secularization may be removing differences between religious traditions in their orientation toward some of the sciences, without erasing faith altogether. Testing that hypothesis is certainly within the scope of cultural science.

A few intellectual critiques of AI can be found on the website of *The New Atlantis*, a publication that Wikipedia suggests is "written from a social conservative stance which utilizes religion," although it is not explicitly faith-oriented.[9] For example, in 2009 the then editor, Ari Schulman, wrote an article titled "Why Minds Are Not Like Computers," effectively calling "artificial intelligence" a false concept, although he did not do so by claiming that human minds are the connection between the world we perceive and the immortal human souls that religious people believe we are.[10]

---

[7] Weber, M. 1930. *The Protestant Ethic and the Spirit of Capitalism*. New York: Scribner; Merton, R.K. 1970. *Science, Technology, and Society in Seventeenth-Century England*. New York, NY: Harper and Row.

[8] Mori, M. 1981. *The Buddha in the Robot*. Tokyo: Kosei.

[9] en.wikipedia.org/wiki/The_New_Atlantis_(journal)

[10] Schulman, A.N. 2009. "Why Minds Are Not Like Computers." *The New Atlantis*, www.thenewatlantis.com/publications/why-minds-are-not-like-computers

Rather more articles criticizing AI are published or linked at Technocracy.com, an organization explicitly against *technocracy*, which is dictatorship by engineers, having a religious heart but not using theology as its main weapon. The brief autobiography of editor Patrick Wood sketches the complexity: "An economist by education, a financial analyst and writer by profession and an American Constitutionalist by choice, Wood maintains a Biblical world view and has deep historical insights into the modern attacks on sovereignty, property rights and personal freedom."[11]

An interview-based article by Jen Copestake for the BBC reported that Pope Francis of the Roman Catholic Church had approved a partnership "with Microsoft to offer an international prize on ethics and artificial intelligence," analyzing it in the Buddhist–Christian disagreement about the sacred nature of the human soul. The article cites Hiroshi Ishiguro, a Japanese robot scientist in the tradition of Masahiro Mori, as predicting humanity might no longer be biological when robotic AI develops sufficiently. Then Copestake summarizes an interview with Archbishop Vincenzo Paglia, president of the Pontifical Academy for Life, which plans a major meeting to discuss AI: "'This dream is a terrible dream,' adding that it was 'impossible' to divide the body and soul. 'The flesh is the body with the soul and the soul is a spirit with flesh,' he asserted." With respect to the more immediate meaning of artificial intelligence,

> "We have underlined the importance of technical research, this is a really good gift that God gave to us," Archbishop Paglia says. "But when we become similar to computers, we immediately see conflicts, dangers, inequalities and sometimes a terrible slavery with the other," he says.[12]

From a Protestant point of view, the Ethics and Religious Liberty Commission of the Southern Baptist Convention recently issued a report introduced by this principle:

---

[11] www.technocracy.news/about
[12] Copestake, J. 2019. "How Pope Francis Could Shape the Future of Robotics." *BBC*, March 24, 2019, www.bbc.com/news/technology-47668476

In light of existential questions posed anew by the emergent technology of artificial intelligence (AI), we affirm that God has given us wisdom to approach these issues in light of Scripture and the gospel message. Christians must not fear the future or any technological development because we know that God is, above all, sovereign over history, and that nothing will ever supplant the image of God in which human beings are created. We recognize that AI will allow us to achieve unprecedented possibilities, while acknowledging the potential risks posed by AI if used without wisdom and care. We desire to equip the church to proactively engage the field of AI, rather than responding to these issues after they have already affected our communities.[13]

In this area of great significance for humanity, such sensitive issues cannot be avoided, but must be addressed with care and respect. Perhaps the world needs a diversity of conceptualizations and design principles for socially significant information technologies, avoiding the metaphor of "artificial intelligence," and focusing instead on specific technologies that are defined individually and serve the values of particular cultures.

2. Artificial stupidity may be the widespread result if excessive enthusiasm for AI causes governments and corporations to automate their services using inferior methods.

Readers will be familiar with one of the most obvious but complex examples, automatic telephone information systems, typically used by service corporations to reduce the cost of providing information to customers. Often including some simple speech recognition AI, but usually employing simple tree-branch algorithms, the system may start by asking the customer which of several issues they wish to deal with, for example, paying a bill versus establishing a new account versus getting some repair

---

[13] The Ethics and Religious Liberty Commission of the Southern Baptist Convention, "Artificial Intelligence: An Evangelical Statement of Principles," April 11, 2019, erlc.com/resource-library/statements/artificial-intelligence-an-evangelical-statement-of-principles

work done. The challenge comes when the customer's need does not fit the often simplistic category system designed into the software. A comparable example that emphasizes more obviously the pressures to deploy a simplistic system is technical assistance for online computer games. With tens or hundreds of thousands of players, the game company would need to double its prices, thus losing potentially all its customers, if it offered easy telephone or text chat conversation with human employees. So if there is a phone number, it merely plays a recording telling the customer to go to the website, where there are branch trees of problems and solutions, or a forum where often confused players suggest solutions to each other. Adding a little feeble AI, tabulating, for example, co-occurrence of words in what the customer is saying could be either smart or stupid, depending upon the practical nature of the technical problems people were facing.

The currently most discussed emerging application of AI in public life is automatic vehicle driving, yet technology journalist Will Knight reported: "The first pedestrian death leads some to ask whether the industry is moving too fast to deploy the technology."[14] Decades ago, it was possible to imagine a division of highway infrastructure into two separate systems, local and city roads where humans would drive their cars in the traditional way, and limited-access highways where the roads themselves included smart sensors and the cars would always drive themselves. But that would have required heavy infrastructure investment in smart highways, and even today governments have limited interest in providing costly but effective infrastructure—not having the funds apparently even to fill the potholes. So smart cars are evolving in several ways, including even just systems to control lane changing. However, customs, laws, and local physical conditions affecting lane changing are not uniform. In *Consumer Reports*, Keith Barry wrote,

---

[14] Knight, W. 2018. "What Uber's Fatal Accident could mean for the Autonomous-Car Industry." *MIT Technology Review*, March 19, 2018, www.technologyreview.com/s/610574/what-ubers-fatal-accident-could-mean-for-the-autonomous-car-industry

Dorothy Glancy, a law professor at Santa Clara University School of Law in California who focuses on transportation and automation, told CR that making sure that automation is programmed to obey traffic laws is one of the many legal concerns that will crop up as vehicle automation increases. "One of the issues we lawyers are looking at is the obligation of autonomous vehicles to obey all traffic laws where the vehicle is being used," she said. "That can get tricky when there are variations from area to area, even within a state—for example, municipal speed limits."[15]

3. The AI fad is drawing attention away from the humanities and social sciences, which are much more important in creating a new civilization that is both peaceful and creative.

Based on extensive data about American university students, Benjamin Schmidt reported that the humanities are in crisis:

Almost every humanities field has seen a rapid drop in majors: History is down about 45 percent from its 2007 peak, while the number of English majors has fallen by nearly half since the late 1990s. Student majors have dropped, rapidly, at a variety of types of institutions. Declines have hit almost every field in the humanities ... and related social sciences, they have not stabilized with the economic recovery, and they appear to reflect a new set of student priorities.[16]

Several explanations have been offered by a diversity of scholars and journalists, including student concerns about what jobs their college majors may prepare them for, and the heavy promotion of natural science and engineering by companies and governments. Some writers have argued

---

[15] www.consumerreports.org/autonomous-driving/tesla-navigate-on-autopilot-automatic-lane-change-requires-significant-driver-intervention

[16] Schmidt, B. 2018. "The Humanities Are in Crisis." *The Atlantic*, August 23, 2018, www.theatlantic.com/ideas/archive/2018/08/the-humanities-face-a-crisisof-confidence/567565

that the negative trend may be an illusion or does not describe what is happening in all nations.[17] Others seek strategies to reverse the trend.[18] Readers who would be interested in examining the trends closely can access frequently updated data from sites such as the Humanities Indicators project of the American Academy of Arts and Sciences, for example, seeing that English literature BA degrees have declined while those for communications have increased.[19] That observation fits the theory that a new cultural science is emerging.

However, in different but discernable ways from nation to nation, the social sciences have struggled for decades to find effective roles in society. The history of recent decades in the United States is rather familiar to me. I entered Harvard graduate school to study sociology immediately after the ambitious Social Relations Department began to disintegrate. It was an amalgam of sociology, cultural anthropology, social psychology, and a somewhat flexible area of clinical or personality psychology.[20] Logically, these fields could have united, but after a quarter century of trying, they could not find a set of objective research methods or a theory that would unify them. Over the years, I have often written about the challenges faced by the multiple competing schools of thought in social psychology and came to this difficult conclusion: Every plausible social psychology theory is true, but only under conditions that are difficult if not impossible to specify.

Subsequently, while earning my tenure at the University of Washington, I paid close attention when a colleague, sociological social psychologist Otto Larsen, went on detail to the National Science Foundation to manage the social and behavioral science programs, the predecessor of today's Directorate for Social, Behavioral, and Economic Sciences. That

---

[17] Mandler, P. "Rise of the Humanities," *Aeon*, aeon.co/essays/the-humanities-are-booming-only-the-professors-can-t-see-it

[18] Dhoul, T. "How Can Universities 'Sell' Arts & Humanities Degrees?" *QS*, www.qs.com/how-can-universities-sell-arts-humanities-degrees

[19] humanitiesindicators.org/content/indicatorDoc.aspx?i=9

[20] Bainbridge, W.S. 2012. "The Harvard Department of Social Relations." In *Leadership in Science and Technology*, ed. W.S. Bainbridge, 496–503. Thousand Oaks, California: Sage.

was right when in 1981 the Reagan administration sought to "zero-out" federal funding for the social sciences, adding existential crises to the cultural crises that were already raging.[21] A decade later, Larsen gently recalled that painful episode in a poetically titled book, *Milestones and Millstones: Social Science at the National Science Foundation, 1945-1991*.[22] One simplistic yet not entirely inaccurate analysis would start with the premise that sociology was an outgrowth of the European socialist movement and is resolutely left-wing, which ignores the fact that many classic theories were politically somewhat conservative, such as those of Talcott Parsons, the creator and leader of Harvard's Social Relations Department. Today, we can set aside those historic struggles and recognize that ideally social science would include schools of thought that harmonized with the full range of political and other cultural strands that weave together in our complex global society.

Political conservatives have also often sought to reduce government funding for the arts and humanities, I would suggest for two cogent reasons. First, at this point in the history of western civilization, conservative cultures are largely religious, not merely biblical but comprising the music, architecture, artworks, and sermons that thrive in houses of worship. Since secular laws prohibit public investment in religious arts, conservatives could well argue that governments should not invest in the competing secular arts either. Second, the popular arts are largely commercial, seemingly trivial to both academics and conservatives alike, and amply funded by the distribution companies. However, today's media are heavily technological, and thus benefitting from advances in computer and information technology, which governments seem very happy to fund. Furthermore, we are entering not merely a postmodern but posthistorical period of time, in which innovation requires cultural exploration rather than robot space probes.

---

[21] McCartney, J.L. 1984. "Setting Priorities for Research: New Politics for the Social Sciences." *The Sociological Quarterly* 25, no. 4, pp. 437–455.

[22] Larsen, O.N. 1992. *Milestones and Millstones: Social Science at the National Science Foundation, 1945–1991*. New Brunswick, New Jersey: Transaction Publishers.

In the wake of the devastating cuts to its social science programs, early in 1984, NSF held a very unusual event, consisting of roundtables in which representatives of the agency's programs discussed the nature of scientific progress with a leading scholar who was well prepared to focus the debate upon a significant perspective. Philosopher Stephen Toulmin led the group titled "Pluralism and Responsibility in Post-Modern Science," representing the relativistic view that many areas of scientific research were not seeking objective truth, but ideas and innovations that could enhance specific cultures and subcultures. To be sure, postmodernism is politically controversial, and taxpayers of diverse ideologies would resent having their money "wasted" on what they considered to be falsehoods. Such thoughts were very much in the mind of Otto Larsen, when he asked Toulmin questions that we may ask ourselves today[23]:

> While post-modern science as you define it is pluralistic, it seems to me also to entail larger and larger units of scientific concern. Post-modern science seems to be anti-disciplinary. Is that a reasonable conclusion?

> Do you contend that when the post-modern sciences finally emerge they will be very pluralistic, will not involve a unifying theory, will not have a great deal of commonality in methodology, and that the agenda of the sciences will be very diverse?

> Is there anything in the knowledge game itself that can help make choices in the allocation of resources among the several sciences? Can science address the question of priorities, or must that be based on an external set of factors?

These questions may not have simple answers, because they concern the convergence–divergence dynamic, at a watershed in the development of human knowledge when new realms may no longer exist to be discovered, but must therefore be created.

---

[23] Toulmin, S.E. 1985. "Pluralism and Responsibility in Post-Modern Science." *Science, Technology, & Human Values* 10, no. 1, pp. 28–37, pp. 34–35.

4. As in the earlier case of the spaceflight social movement, which gave us ICBM nuclear weapons rather than colonies on Mars, AI is magnifying the danger of war in an increasingly conflicted world.

Many of the organization reports and news articles posted on the AIM Facebook group concerned worries about military misuse of artificial intelligence, even sometimes defining any use as misuse. Prominent in the mass media were stories about weaponized chatbots, deep fake videos, and recommender AI systems designed to mislead people during covert cyberwar or politics.[24] The ultimate solution may be abandonment of the notion that news media can be objective, hovering above all subcultures, and placing trust only in people we know personally and have carefully learned to trust, the *local opinion leaders* that were so prominent in sociology half a century ago, local meaning either geographic neighbors or fellow subculture members. The potential power of local critics was clearly illustrated by the 2018 debate between the Google corporation and a group of its employees who wanted to stop its development of

---

[24] Neudert, L.M. 2018. "Future Elections may be Swayed by Intelligent, Weaponized Chatbots: The AI Advances that Brought you Alexa are Teaching Propaganda How To Talk." *MIT Technology Review*, August 22, 2018, www.technologyreview.com/s/611832/future-elections-may-be-swayed-by-intelligent-weaponized-chatbots; Roose, K. 2018. "Here Come the Fake Videos, Too: Artificial Intelligence Video Tools Make it Relatively Easy to Put One Person's Face on Another Person's Body with Few Traces of Manipulation. I Tried It on Myself. What Could Go Wrong?" *The New York Times*, March 4, 2018, www.nytimes.com/2018/03/04/technology/fake-videos-deepfakes.html; Breland, A. 2018. "Lawmakers worry about rise of fake video technology," *The Hill*, February 19, 2018,   thehill.com/policy/technology/374320-lawmakers-worry-about-rise-of-fake-video-technology.

military drones.[25] A clear and concise statement of major issues is the Lethal Autonomous Weapons Pledge of the Future of Life Institute:

> Artificial intelligence (AI) is poised to play an increasing role in military systems. There is an urgent opportunity and necessity for citizens, policymakers, and leaders to distinguish between acceptable and unacceptable uses of AI. In this light, we the undersigned agree that the decision to take a human life should never be delegated to a machine. There is a moral component to this position, that we should not allow machines to make life-taking decisions for which others—or nobody—will be culpable. There is also a powerful pragmatic argument: lethal autonomous weapons, selecting and engaging targets without human intervention, would be dangerously destabilizing for every country and individual. Thousands of AI researchers agree that by removing the risk, attributability, and difficulty of taking human lives, lethal autonomous weapons could become powerful instruments of violence and oppression, especially when linked to surveillance and data

[25] Conger, K., and D. Cameron. 2018. "Google Is Helping the Pentagon Build AI for Drones." *Gizmodo*, March 6, 2018, gizmodo.com/google-is-helping-the-pentagon-build-ai-for-drones-1823464533; Eckersley, P., and C. Cohn. 2018. "Google Should Not Help the U.S. Military Build Unaccountable AI Systems." *Electronic Frontier Foundation*, April 5, 2018, www.eff.org/deeplinks/2018/04/should-google-really-be-helping-us-military-build-ai-systems; Harwell, D. 2018. "Google to Drop Pentagon AI contract After Employee Objections to the 'Business of War,'" *Washington Post*, June 1, 2018, www.washingtonpost.com/news/the-switch/wp/2018/06/01/google-to-drop-pentagon-ai-contract-after-employees-called-it-the-business-of-war; Knight, W. 2018. "Don't be AI-vil: Google Says Its Algorithms Will Do No Harm: Google has Created a Set of Principles for its Artificial-Intelligence Researchers to live by—and they Prohibit Weapons Technology." *MIT Technology Review*, June 7, 2018, www.technologyreview.com/s/611379/dont-be-ai-vil-google-says-its-algorithms-will-do-no-harm; International Committee for Robot Arms Control, Knight, W. 2018. "Open Letter in Support of Google Employees and Tech Workers: Researchers in Support of Google Employees: Google Should Withdraw from Project Maven and Commit to not Weaponizing its Technology." *ICRAC*, June 25, 2018, www.icrac.net/open-letter-in-support-of-google-employees-and-tech-workers

systems. Moreover, lethal autonomous weapons have characteristics quite different from nuclear, chemical and biological weapons, and the unilateral actions of a single group could too easily spark an arms race that the international community lacks the technical tools and global governance systems to manage. Stigmatizing and preventing such an arms race should be a high priority for national and global security.[26]

The one obvious flaw in this pledge is that it is limited to lethal systems that are autonomous, when a wider statement would demand the destruction of all nuclear weapons and the intercontinental ballistic missiles that can deliver them anywhere on this poor planet. In a sense, once a missile has been launched by humans, it is always autonomous, using elaborate control systems to aim itself toward its humanly selected target. I was recently discussing with colleagues via email a Federal Engagement in Artificial Intelligence Standards Workshop organized by the National Institute of Standards and Technology (NIST), based on this premise:

> Timely and fit-for-purpose AI technical standards—whether developed by national or international organizations—will play a crucial role in the development and deployment of AI technologies, and will be essential in building trust and confidence about AI technologies and for achieving economies of scale.[27]

I could not resist linking to an online definition of *standard*: "'flag or other conspicuous object to serve as a rallying point for a military force,' from shortened form of Old French *estandart* 'military standard, banner.'"[28] So, standards are elements of culture, even metaphors for loyal subculture membership, although in cases such as inches and centimeters, they may sometimes be translatable.

---

[26] futureoflife.org/lethal-autonomous-weapons-pledge
[27] www.nist.gov/news-events/events/2019/05/federal-engagement-artificial-intelligence-standards-workshop
[28] www.etymonline.com/word/standard

5. It is reasonable to worry that AI would greatly reduce the need for human workers, thus causing a surge in unemployment, given that the principle of creative destruction that earlier created more new jobs does not apply once technology is able to duplicate fundamental human abilities.

Complaints that robots and other AI applications are causing human unemployment or degrading the work experience of employees may be true in some cases but false in others, while often they are based in political disagreements about how modern economies should be organized. An article of faith in economics for decades has been the *creative destruction* thesis that new technologies do kill old kinds of jobs, to the inconvenience of older workers poorly positioned to learn new skills, but they almost invariably create more new jobs because they increase the size of the economy.[29] However, in their 2011 book, *Race against the Machine*, Erik Brynjolfsson and Andrew McAfee described a very complex dynamic in which many humans, perhaps even a majority, could lose that race.[30] Since then, many critics and social scientists have debated the facts about what is really happening, and what if anything could be done to mitigate the loss of jobs or income, without a clear result.[31]

Economists are quite aware that many factors are at work. Should harm or benefit be measured in terms of the employment rate among those both holding and seeking jobs, or more broadly among adults in general? Or should the measure be the median annual income of

[29] Schumpeter, J. 1942. *Capitalism, Socialism, and Democracy*. New York: Harper; Elliott, J.E. 1980. "Marx and Schumpeter on Capitalism's Creative Destruction: A Comparative Restatement." *Quarterly Journal of Economics* 95, pp. 45–68.

[30] Brynjolfsson, E., and A. McAfee. 2011. *Race Against the Machine*. Digital Frontier Press, Lexington, Massachusetts.

[31] Kristal, T. 2013. "The Capitalist Machine: Computerization, Workers' Power, and the Decline in Labor's Share Within U.S. Industries." *American Sociological Review* 78, no. 3, pp. 361–389; Elsby, M.W.L., B. Hobijn, and A. Sahin. 2013. "The Decline of the U.S. Labor Share." *Brookings Papers on Economic Activity* 2, pp. 1–52; Frey, C.B., and M.A. Osborne. 2013. *The Future of Employment: How Susceptible are Jobs to Computerization?*. Oxford, United Kingdom: Oxford Martin.

households, or the percent near or below the culturally determined poverty line? Information technologies can increase unemployment in a particular society either by transferring jobs to local machines or by transferring jobs to another society where workers' incomes and freedoms are weaker. Globalization may be to the benefit of the most technologically advanced nations, but whether this should be measured by the international balance of payments or the well-being of the least educated groups in the population is open to debate. Educational institutions promote themselves through rhetoric that any social problems suffered by disadvantaged groups can be solved by making sure they get more education. It is politically incorrect, but perhaps factually correct, to suggest that many individuals and subcultures cannot effectively compete in a world dominated by information technologies. To address this vast array of issues, cultural science may need to converge with economics, perhaps in the ways in which economics often collaborates with cognitive science.

In an earlier book in this series, *Virtual Local Manufacturing Communities: Online Simulations of Future Workshop Systems*, I suggested that distributed manufacturing offers the promise of bringing jobs back to local communities, producing goods that are personalized or harmonize with distinctive cultures, and thereby reversing significant aspects of the globalization that has dominated in recent years.[32] Large corporations may still have important roles to play, but in collaboration with local workshops, for example, providing machinery, software, databases of designs, toolbased AI that effectively increases the expertise of local workers, and communication media suitable for a diverse and dynamic workforce. Many other kinds of innovation may be needed to assure that the optimism of the creative destruction thesis will be correct, but local manufacturing, of artworks as well as equipment, demonstrates the potential economic significance of cultural science.

6. Automation concentrates power in a small number of large corporations and a technical elite, increasing inequality across the social classes.

---

[32] Bainbridge, W.S. 2019. *Virtual Local Manufacturing Communities: Online Simulations of Future Workshop Systems*. Business Expert Press.

Residents of democratic nations like to think that democracy is the modern form of government, and dictatorships are anachronistic reflections of primitive systems of dominance by kings and emperors. But anyone who has read the history of the classical societies of Greece and Rome would know this is a far too simplistic faith. Athens and Rome began as republics, evolving from the chaotic social structures of the Indo-European invaders of Greece and Italy that had arisen in the equivalent of a Wild West frontier, then decayed into tyrannies in the hands of leaders like Alexander the Great, Julius Caesar, and the politically named Augustus Caesar. A more moderate but possibly also excessively optimistic viewpoint is the Iron Law of Oligarchy proposed over a century ago by Robert Michels that well-established societies will oscillate between near-democracy and near-tyranny, never achieving perfect justice, because the leaders of reform movements will use them to their own advantage, becoming a new elite.[33] A naive yet not unintelligent hypothesis is that human freedom is best preserved by keeping it local, housed in city-states like the early Athens and Rome.

The century-old Frontier Thesis of Frederick Jackson Turner suggests that freedom requires the existence of a disruptive frontier like the Wild West, which supported democracy even in more settled regions through its dynamic effects on social and economic networks.[34] Vannevar Bush, the original instigator of NSF, asserted that *science is the endless frontier*, yet returns on investment in several areas of science and engineering are diminishing.[35] Computer scientists traditionally proclaimed the general applicability of *Moore's Law*, proposed by Gordon Moore in 1965, that the complexity of electronic circuits doubles every year or two.[36] More recently, *Eroom's Law* has been proposed, spelling Gordon's last name backward, that progress in pharmaceutical development has been declin-

[33] Michels, R. 1915. *Political Parties*. New York, NY: Hearst's International Library.

[34] Turner, F.J. 1920. *The Frontier in American History*. New York: Holt.

[35] Bush, V. 1945. *Science, the Endless Frontier*. Washington, D.C.: U. S. Government Printing Office.

[36] Moore, G.E. 1965. "Cramming More Components onto Integrated Circuits." *Electronics* 38, no. 8, pp. 114–117.

ing, perhaps inexorably.[37] Today the *Star Trek* notion that space is the final frontier becomes worrisome, as we approach half a century since anybody has visited the moon. After documenting the deceleration of scientific progress in recent years and the increasing costs of discovery, Patrick Collison and Michael Nielsen supported the

> optimistic view is that science is an endless frontier, and we will continue to discover and even create entirely new fields, with their own fundamental questions. If we see a slowing today, it is because science has remained too focused on established fields, where it's becoming ever harder to make progress. We hope the future will see a more rapid proliferation of new fields, giving rise to major new questions. This is an opportunity for science to accelerate.[38]

Cultural science could become the most progressive new field, notably achieving the functions of a traditional frontier by different means, the diversification of cultural structures.

7. Whether through privacy violations, oppressive propaganda personalized to be most effective in controlling individual victims, or automatic infliction of punishments, AI may be used intentionally by governments to reduce the freedom of their citizens.

Sociologist Barry Schwartz explained that society is a dynamic system, characterized by both social cohesion (intimacy) and social separation (privacy), which implies that different cultures and subcultures will develop different privacy policies.[39] Indeed, in the Schwartz model, pri-

---

[37] Scannell, J.W., A. Blanckley, H. Boldon, and B. Warrington. 2012. "Diagnosing the Decline in Pharmaceutical R&D Efficiency." *Nature Reviews* 11, pp. 191–200.

[38] Collison, P., and M. Nielsen. 2018. "Science Is Getting Less Bang for Its Buck." *The Atlantic*, November 16, 2018, www.theatlantic.com/science/archive/2018/11/diminishing-returns-science/575665

[39] Schwartz, B. 1968. "The Social Psychology of Privacy." *American Journal of Sociology* 73, no. 6, pp. 741–752.

vacy means being open to members of one's own intimate group, but closed to members of other groups. An example relevant to the themes of this book is a guild named Science that I organized for the May 2008 conference held in *World of Warcraft*, where avatars representing 120 scholars and students met on each of three days to discuss the social science of early online communities, encouraged and publicized by the highly respectable *Science* magazine.[40] Creating a guild gave us a private text chat channel that nonmembers could not access, so those passing strangers who saw 120 avatars standing on the hilly seacoast east of the Orc city of Orgrimmar would have had no idea what we were doing or what real-world identities our avatars had.[41] Each session was led by a panel of four or five experts, who had posted on our private wiki a list of questions to be addressed, each of them having prepared text communicating their thoughts, but all 120 participants could add text which I automatically downloaded and assembled into two chapters of the conventional paper book of conference proceedings that was published later.[42] So one rather effective privacy mechanism seldom studied by scientists is simply creation of closed computer-mediated social groups, with some predefined or evolving authority structure, including the ability of leaders to expel members who misbehaved.

During the first six months of 2019 when the AIM Facebook group was especially active, it shared many news articles about privacy concerns related to face recognition systems employing the form of artificial intelligence often called computer vision. At the website of *MIT Technology Review* on December 6, 2018, critical tech journalist Will Knight published an article with this subtitle: "The research institute AI Now has identified facial recognition as a key challenge for society and policymakers

[40] Bohannon, J. 2008. "Scientists, We Need Your Swords!" *Science* 320, no. 5874, p. 312. science.sciencemag.org/content/320/5874/312.2

[41] archive.org/details/Science_WoW_Conference_9May2008_gathering

[42] Bainbridge, W.S. ed., 2010. *Online Worlds: Convergence of the Real and the Virtual.* London: Springer.

—but is it too late?"[43] He mentioned two topics we were familiar with, the bias against minorities in the use of facial recognition in police work and the aggressive use of many advanced technologies by the government of China on its population, but we had not yet seen the new AI Now report. Supported by an extensive analysis, it offers 10 main recommendations, including this rather critical one: "The AI industry urgently needs new approaches to governance. As this report demonstrates, internal governance structures at most technology companies are failing to ensure accountability for AI systems."[44] As much as we might agree that governments should develop standards for the application of new technologies that may have harmful as well as beneficial consequences, in the current world governments have lost considerable legitimacy, and there is no one acknowledged adjudicator for ethics.

The AIM Facebook group contemplated many news articles and commentaries about the use of AI and other advanced computer technologies in China, as tools for building a society based on principles very different from those enshrined in the Constitution of the United States. We are in no position to judge the factual accuracy of the reports and should avoid speculating about the causes and consequences of the new technology policies. These are vast and hugely important topics for future cultural science research. Yet in a chapter of an earlier book I explored the Chinese massively multiplayer online game *Perfect World* from the perspective that Chinese culture has long sought to base itself on formal principles managed by an elite class of intellectuals, and this seems to apply to the current moment in China's vast history.[45]

---

[43] Will Knight: Facial recognition has to be regulated to protect the public, says AI report: The research institute AI Now has identified facial recognition as a key challenge for society and policymakers - but is it too late?" *MIT Technology Review*, December 6, 2018, www.technologyreview.com/s/612552/facial-recognition-has-to-be-regulated-to-protect-the-public-says-ai-report

[44] Whittaker, M., K. Crawford, R. Dobbe, G. Fried, E. Kaziunas, V. Mathur, S.M. West, R. Richardson, J. Schultz, and O. Schwartz. 2018. "AI Now Report 2018." AI Now Institute, New York University, December 2018, p. 4, ainowinstitute.org/AI_Now_2018_Report.pdf

[45] Bainbridge, W.S. 2014. *An Information Technology Surrogate for Religion: The Veneration of Deceased Family in Online Games*, 55–68. London: Palgrave Macmillan.

I remember my Chinese aunt, the daughter of a high-level official in the prerevolutionary government, saying: "Bill, we Chinese are not religious! We are Confucian." Whether Maoist equals Confucian, or what term such as Cybernetic should be applied today, the goal seems to be a logic-based uniform culture. The titles of four news articles shared through AIM dramatize the highly dynamic situation: (1) "Deep Learning 'Godfather' Bengio Worries About China's Use of AI"[46]; (2) "One Month, 500,000 Face Scans: How China Is Using A.I. to Profile a Minority"[47]; (3) "China's new 'social credit system' turns Orwell's '1984' into reality"[48]; (4) "China's robot censors crank up as Tiananmen anniversary nears."[49] The use of facial recognition intentionally to track ethnic minorities has been reported repeatedly, for example, an article in *Forbes* asserting: "These systems have been honed in Xinjiang, an unconstrained high-tech surveillance laboratory where the industrial-scale oppression of the Muslim Uighur population has created a belated wave of international condemnation in recent months."[50] In a society with absolutely uniform norms and beliefs, cultural science will be irrelevant. But in any real society, it can take on great significance.

---

[46] Kahn, J. 2019. "Deep Learning 'Godfather' Bengio Worries About China's Use of AI." *Bloomberg*, February 2, 2019, finance.yahoo.com/news/deep-learning-godfather-bengio-worries-060100282.html

[47] Mozur, P. 2019. "One Month, 500,000 Face Scans: How China Is Using A.I. to Profile a Minority." *New York Times*, April 14, 2019, www.nytimes.com/2019/04/14/technology/china-surveillance-artificial-intelligence-racial-profiling.html

[48] Mosher, S.W. 2019. "China's New 'Social Credit System' Turns Orwell's '1984' into Reality." *New York Post*, May 18, 2019, nypost.com/2019/05/18/chinas-new-social-credit-system-turns-orwells-1984-into-reality

[49] Cadell, C. 2019. "China's Robot Censors Crank up as Tiananmen Anniversary Nears." *Reuters*, May 26, 2019, www.reuters.com/article/us-china-tiananmen-censorship-idUSKCN1SW03Y

[50] Doffman, Z. 2019. "China Is Using Facial Recognition To Track Ethnic Minorities, Even In Beijing." *Forbes*, May 3, 2019, www.forbes.com/sites/zakdoffman/2019/05/03/china-new-data-breach-exposes-facial-recognition-and-ethnicity-tracking-in-beijing

8. Despite the excessive dramatization of AI's dangers in popular movies like *Terminator* (1984) and *The Matrix* (1999), development of Artificial General Intelligence could conceivably result in the extinction of humanity.

At the risk of being accused of sarcasm, we could end this book in this sentence by suggesting that Artificial General Intelligence will not be developed for many years, so later generations will be in a better position to deal with it. However, for once, the trivial is more important than the significant. Like the term *standard*, *significant* is a quasi-synonym for *metaphor* or *symbol*, as an online etymology service defines it: "'having a meaning,' from Latin *significantem* (nominative *significans*, present participle of *significare* 'make known, indicate') (see *signify*)."[51] The surrealistic image of an autonomous war robot or Terminator attacking us is a sign that AI can be dangerous.[52] But the real danger is that many tiny AI worms could gradually eat away at human freedom, transforming our society into a Matrix of algorithms, imprisoning humans, and causing the slow death of cultural creativity. It is not surprising that many critics and even corporate leaders have advocated transparency in AI, so that people

---

[51] www.etymonline.com/word/significant

[52] "Autonomy in Weapon Systems." *Department of Defense*, May 8, 2017, www.esd.whs.mil/Portals/54/Documents/DD/issuances/dodd/300009p.pdf; Brundage, M., and S. Avin., eds. 2019. "The Malicious Use of Artificial Intelligence: Forecasting, Prevention, and Mitigation." *Future of Humanity Institute*, Oxford University. maliciousaireport.com; Tucker, P. 2019. "Pentagon Seeks a List of Ethical Principles for Using AI in War." Defense One, January 4, 2019, www.defenseone.com/technology/2019/01/pentagon-seeks-list-ethical-principles-using-ai-war/153940; Ayed, N. 2018. "'Very urgent': Activists Want Global Treaty to Ban Killer Robots by 2019: Discussions Resume in Geneva Tuesday on Lethal Autonomous Weapons Systems." *CBC News*, April 10, 2018 www.cbc.ca/news/world/killer-robots-lethal-autonomous-weapons-discussions-1.4611205

will always be able to understand, and thus to manage safely, what the algorithms are doing.[53]

Conclusion

In October 2016, in the last days of the Obama administration, the U.S. government published *The National Artificial Intelligence Research and Development Strategic Plan* that advocated heavy investment in AI research, following seven strategic priorities, including "Understand and address the ethical, legal, and societal implications of AI." In June 2019 the subsequent Trump administration issued a revised plan, adding an emphasis on partnership between government and industry, but retaining the key text concerning ethics, including principles that would support the vigorous development of cultural science:

> Research in this area can benefit from multidisciplinary perspectives that involve experts from computer science, social and behavioral sciences, ethics, biomedical science, psychology, economics, law, and policy research... Ethical issues vary according to culture, religion, and beliefs. However, acceptable ethics reference frameworks can be developed to guide AI system reasoning and

---

[53] Captain, S. 2016. "We Don't Always Know What AI Is Thinking—And That Can Be Scary: IBM's Artificial Intelligence Chief Calls for Building a Window into the Inner Workings of Algorithms So We Understand What AI is up to." *Fast Company*, November 15, 2016, www.fastcompany.com/3064368/we-dont-always-know-what-ai-is-thinking-and-that-can-be-scary; Banavar, G. 2016. "Learning to Trust Artificial Intelligence Systems: Accountability, Compliance and Ethics in the Age of Smart Machines." *Somers*, NY: IBM Global Services, 2016, www.alain-bensoussan.com/wp-content/uploads/2017/06/34348524.pdf

decision-making, in order to explain and justify its conclusions and actions.[54]

Exactly how to integrate sophisticated information technologies into human life, whether or not we call them *artificial intelligence*, will require extensive and diverse research. Unless some modern Moses can bring down a divine computer chip from a newly discovered mountain top, cultures and subcultures will need the power and insight to adapt technology to their distinctive norms and values. This will require deep cultural science of the technology, the technology's producers and users, but most importantly the people who choose whether or how to accept each distinctive innovation into their own lives.

---

[54] Networking and Information Technology Research and Development Subcommittee of the National Science and Technology Council, *The National Artificial Intelligence Research and Development Strategic Plan*, 26–27. October 2016, www.nitrd.gov/pubs/national_ai_rd_strategic_plan.pdf; Select Committee on Artificial Intelligence of the National Science & Technology Council, *The National Artificial Intelligence Research and Development Strategic Plan: 2018 Update*, 20–21, June 2019, www.nitrd.gov/pubs/National-AI-RD-Strategy-2019-printer.pdf

About the Author

William Sims Bainbridge has written 30 academic books and about 300 articles or book chapters, in areas such as technological innovation, social movements, and modern culture. Beginning in the 1980s, he programmed much educational and research software incorporating machine learning or rule-based artificial intelligence, and has edited encyclopedias on human-computer interaction and leadership in science and technology. He represented the social and information sciences in organizing the Converging Technologies conferences of the U.S. government, which resulted in 11 edited volumes that sought to unite nanotechnology, biotechnology, information technology, and cognitive science. He currently serves as a program director in the Information and Intelligent Systems division of the National Science Foundation.

Index

OTHER TITLES IN THE COLLABORATIVE INTELLIGENCE COLLECTION

- *The Interconnected Individual* by Hunter Hastings and Jeff Saperstein
- *T-Shaped Professionals* by Yassi Moghaddam and Haluk Demirkan
- *Virtual Local Manufacturing Communities* by William Sims Bainbridge
- *Advancing Talent Development* by Philip Gardner and Heather N. Maietta
- *The Future of Work* by Yassi Moghaddam and Heather Yurko

Announcing the Business Expert Press Digital Library

Concise e-books business students need for classroom and research

This book can also be purchased in an e-book collection by your library as

- a one-time purchase,
- that is owned forever,
- allows for simultaneous readers,
- has no restrictions on printing, and
- can be downloaded as PDFs from within the library community.

Our digital library collections are a great solution to beat the rising cost of textbooks. E-books can be loaded into their course management systems or onto students' e-book readers.
The **Business Expert Press** digital libraries are very affordable, with no obligation to buy in future years. For more information, please visit **www.businessexpertpress.com/librarians**. To set up a trial in the United States, please email **sales@businessexpertpress.com**.

www.ingramcontent.com/pod-product-compliance
Lightning Source LLC
Chambersburg PA
CBHW061216220326
41599CB00025B/4657